EDUCATION
FOR ALL

TALES FROM THE CLASSROOM AND THE PURSUIT OF EQUITABLE REFORM

MITCHELL REESE GREEN

Printed by B.C. Allen Publishing and Tonic Books
144 N 7th St. #525
Brooklyn, NY 11249

Now taking manuscript submissions and book ideas at any stage of the process: submissions@tonicbooks.online

Printed in the United States of America

Editor: Lauren Miller
Cover Design: Najdan Mancic
Interior Design: Megan McCullough

ISBN: 978-1-7371284-7-2 (Paperback)

Endorsements

"Well-written with warmth backed by a philosophy of action."

—Steve Hauk, journalist, playwright, documentary screenwriter, and author of *Steinbeck: The Untold Stories*

"There are books that are written about the classroom, and then there are books that KNOW the classroom. *Education . . . for All: Tales from the Classroom and the Pursuit of Equitable Reform* is a must-read for any teacher looking for insight, experience, and answers to confidently start their career, and a must-read for any seasoned teacher needing inspiration and rejuvenation to remind them why they started teaching in the first place. Green weaves story, humanity, and practical advice seamlessly throughout this important read."

—Julietta Skoog, Ed.S, MA, co-founder of *Sproutable*

"I am a parent of two children, one now in college and one in high school, both of whom attended public schools since kindergarten. Mitchell Green, in his book *Education . . . for All* offers practical, thoughtful, and accessible ideas with the goal of getting the most out of public education. Through his extensive experience and teaching antidotes, Mitchell provides a framework to foster a love of learning in students and a love of teaching in educators. Thought provoking and recommended reading for any parent."

—N. Lea, mother

"*Education . . . for All* provided such a unique perspective on today's education system, what is influencing our children's experience and impacting the outcome. I found Mitchell's insights and personal experiences to be super helpful when thinking about my own children's education."

—Jodie Scott, mother of fifth- and seventh-grade students in public school

This book is dedicated to all children,
their families, educators,
and supporting communities.

Contents

Preface

While I was flat on my back in a Seattle hospital, I entertained the idea of teaching for a living. Persistent back issues had led me to surgery at the age of twenty-eight, and as I made my way through a long recovery period, I realized that I didn't want to return to my career in direct sales. The money was great, and I enjoyed being one of the national sales leaders in my company, but that was not enough incentive for me to stay. So after many hours of contemplation, I decided to explore teaching—and I never looked back.

The perspectives I offer in this book come from direct experience in the classroom and at the building, district, and state levels, plus reading and discussions with others at the national level, all of which have shaped my outlook on the state of our public school system. During my fifteen years of classroom teaching, I mostly taught upper elementary and middle school classes, though I have experience from the kindergarten classroom to post-graduate school. I spent countless hours on building- and district-level committees, and the last seven-plus years of my career I worked in curriculum leadership, where I supported K–12 mathematics instruction for two large districts. I have also worked at the state level on issues of multicultural education, mathematics education, and assessment.

The vast majority of this work took place in diverse, low-income, and "low-performing" schools. My experiences there have fostered a zeal for public education that is grounded in a passion for social justice, truth, and love.

After spending more than twenty years in the teaching profession—which I wholeheartedly enjoyed and still believe in—I am left with two questions:

- **What is the purpose of public education?** Believe it or not, there is no general consensus; even among educators, you'll hear a dozen different answers: To prepare *all* students for college. So we can truly have an educated populace for an informed democratic republic. To foster creativity and knowledge. So kids can learn to read and write. So they have a supervised place to go while parents work. To help them make sense of the world and find their niche in life.

  Each of these answers is valid in its own way. Which leads me to wonder: Does public education need only *one* goal? Can it have several? I don't have an answer, but I do understand the significance of this lack of accord; people are attempting to reform a system when they can't even agree on what purpose(s) said system should serve.

- **Do we believe that *all* children deserve the same learning opportunities and resources, that *all* children can, in fact, learn?** Though many would answer yes, you wouldn't know it as an objective observer in any of the school districts where I have taught. One school can raise over $10,000 in one night for art and language lessons while just five miles away, another school in the same district struggles to get the basics, having to ask parents to provide essentials like tissues and a ream of paper for the copy machine. If we truly believed that all children should have access to the same opportunities—and, at a more fundamental level, that all children are quite capable of learning—then we would address these glaring inequalities.

Our inability to agree on the purpose of public education and our collective resigned acceptance of the inequities inherent in the current system are sabotaging reform efforts. There's not much I, alone, can do about that, other than to prompt reflection and maybe a little conversation, and to shine a light on the children and teachers themselves, on what their lives inside and outside the classroom look like. While politicians, educators, administrators, and even your average citizen are spouting off about reform, it's easy to forget upon whose shoulders the work of these changes so heavily falls: students and teachers.

Many aspects of children's lives affect how well they perform academically—from their morning routine to the journey through neighborhood to school; to what happens in the halls, on the playground, and in the cafeteria; to how well their teacher has been trained; to how the staff in the main office treat them; to how much the principal is engaged in day-to-day school activity; and so much more—not just what happens in the classroom. That's what most people overlook when they propose solutions to improve academic achievement. And inevitably their hopes are dashed because those solutions fail to produce the desired results.

If my years in the teaching profession have taught me anything, it's this: before we pontificate about which textbook, lesson-planning method, reading program, or testing protocol is going to revolutionize education, we need to understand what school is like for the children and adults who learn, teach, and work there every day. This book provides an in-the-trenches perspective on students' journeys through the educational system—the successes, failures, disappointments, joys, tragedies, and a few minor miracles. Read on to get a glimpse of the real world of public schools—and perhaps a few ideas about how we could approach reform with less bluster, more insight, and even greater compassion.

The purpose of this work is to identify the major influences of student learning so that we can gain a holistic perspective on what it will take to enact meaningful, equitable school improvement. Chapter 1 introduces those influences and demonstrates how they interact to affect children; Chapters 2 through 8 discuss each influence in detail; and Chapter 9 suggests possibilities for improving the system and some actions that people can take to fight for positive change.

This book doesn't offer simple answers, or many answers at all. If that's what you are looking for, you are likely to be disappointed.

What you will find here are stories, questions, and facts that hopefully spark informed discussion about how to improve students' lives—personal and academic (because you can't separate the two). I share my experiences with students, other teachers, administration, and parents. I offer my successes and failures, what I have learned about how the public education system works—and doesn't work for students, and how we might go about changing it for the better. For years I encouraged students to allow their voices to be heard, and now I am practicing a bit of what I preached! It is my hope that the following pages will not only give you a glimpse into the day-to-day realities of educating children but also inspire you to demand wholesale reform that provides high-quality, equitable education for *all* children.

Chapter 1

What Influences Student Learning?

Awakenings

It was an inauspicious setting in which to begin my teaching career: a creaky, drafty, decades-old, three-story brick building on a slope with one side overlooking a lake. A major freeway, built long after the school, cut a wide, noisy path thirty yards from the front door. On the side facing the freeway, so much noise permeated the classrooms' large single-pane windows that some teachers had to use microphones to be heard. The school building was under consideration for closure because of low enrollment and badly needed repairs and renovations. Yet despite its decrepit state, it was here, in this Seattle elementary school in 1986, that I discovered my calling.

Within moments of my stint volunteering in a fourth-grade classroom, of seeing and hearing the children, feeling their energy, I knew I belonged. The peace and joy I felt inside—even after a day of observing mundane lessons; managing misbehavior, tears, laughter, and snitching; helping children with assignments; and learning how to use a Ditto machine (ask your parents if you don't know what that is)—was powerful and reassuring; each moment made me eager for the next. And I kept that eagerness throughout the next twenty-four years.

What I did not realize as a young, enthusiastic, slightly naive volunteer was how little the public education system would change in the span of my career. Sure, progress occurred in dribs and drabs—the percentage of students who graduate high school has risen and classrooms now have computers and internet access, for example—but largely the system has lumbered along in much the same way as it always has. We continue to face the same problems: achievement gaps between white and minority students, mediocre academic performance in math and science, high rates of teacher burnout, and inadequate, inconsistent funding, just to name a few. Why?

One problem is that school reform "solutions" tend to follow a piecemeal approach, usually dealing with one factor of student academic achievement, such as standardized testing, without looking at the big picture. There are many interconnected influences, both within and outside schools, that affect how well students perform. For example, it was clear to me on my first day volunteering in that fourth-grade classroom in Seattle just how many influences shaped a student's learning experience (and this is not remotely an exhaustive list):

- The building itself, which was run-down, and the drone of the nearby freeway noise

- Efforts toward integration, including the minority children's miles-long bus ride to the predominantly white neighborhood

- The lack of basic resources like paper and enough books for all students

- The principal who was in the last year of his career and never left his office

- The staff who ranged widely in experience and attitude—from twenty-five-year-old first-year teachers bubbling with enthusiasm to thirty-year veteran teachers looking forward to retirement and radiating an Eeyore-like cloud

- The community inside the school, which was nonexistent—individual classrooms had their own unique cultures, some positive and some not

- The grading procedures, which varied from class to class

- The rigmarole of mandatory testing for all

Failure to acknowledge how these influences affect academic achievement fuels the disconnect between school reform and the reality of what day-to-day life is like inside American classrooms. For example, imagine for a moment that you are volunteering in that fourth-grade class like the one I just described. Every day you and the teacher are responsible for meeting the students' individual needs while also holding the entire class, thirty students, to the same educational standards.

Than is a Vietnamese boy who lives with his mother (who does not speak English) and two sisters in Section 8 housing. His father died when he was an infant. He receives free lunch at school. Than is an intelligent, generally happy child, though in class he frequently talks out of turn and can be disruptive. He struggles with reading and math; his abilities are about two grades behind where they should be.

Sarah is a white girl who lives with her mother and her mother's boyfriend in a one-bedroom apartment (Sarah sleeps on the couch). She sees her father sporadically. At school, she often wears a frown on her face, sometimes bullies other children, and receives reduced lunch prices. While witty and very athletic, she is not confident in her abilities. She performs slightly below grade level for most subjects.

Angela is an African American girl who lives with her parents and one younger sibling in a single-family home. Angela is very bright, a positive leader in the class, and full of joy. She enjoys singing and is quite musically inclined (though the music program at this school has been cut due to lack of funding). Her reading and math skills are at least two to three years ahead of her peers.

The more you think about public education in terms of individual children, it's easy to see the complexity of creating an environment where all students have the opportunities and resources they need to succeed. Simplistic, one-issue approaches to improving student achievement, like adopting new textbooks, will inevitably fail. Will a new book ensure that Than, Sarah, and Angela—children with different emotional and intellectual needs and widely varying abilities—receive a high-caliber education? Sure, new textbooks should be adopted, but we need to be realistic about what an approach like this can reasonably achieve. I can guarantee you that it isn't wholesale improvement in academic performance (despite what textbook publishers promise).

It seems that we've sacrificed taking the time to understand what affects student achievement in favor of taking action, any action that can be perceived as improving children's educational experiences—whether it actually does or not. Maybe it's time we slow down and examine these influences, what they are, and how they interact, so we can tackle school reform with not only clear intention and sufficient knowledge but also a vision for long-term sustainability.

This book examines the seven major influences on learning, where they intersect, and ultimately, how they shape a student's educational journey. Through sharing my experiences with children, staff, and parents, I provide an inside view of what happens in public schools—from how textbooks dictate instruction to how a school's individual culture can affect achievement to how high-stakes testing undermines learning, among other topics. While I do suggest possible actions readers can take to effect positive change, I do not offer easy fixes. Instead, I ask questions and share stories to provoke informed, nuanced conversations about how we can ensure all children—no matter where they live or their background—thrive in public schools.

We'll begin this journey by defining an important term: *curriculum*. To do that, let's take a deep dive into what the beginning of the school year is like, before students even pass through the doors.

Curriculum: What *Does* It Mean?

The school gym was buzzing with chatter about the previous six weeks of summer break. It was early in the morning on a beautiful mid-August Monday. A new school year would begin in a few weeks, and the nearly ninety staff members of two elementary schools were gathered to learn about the new mathematics program the district had adopted. The principals were scurrying around, checking on the coffee and snacks, and stopping to briefly greet staff members. Lively stories of camping, summer courses, beach vacations, books read (or just started), and home projects in various stages of completion were among the topics of conversation.

Virtually everyone came around to talking about the upcoming year. There is a general sense of optimism around this time; teachers tend to be relaxed while discussing room arrangements, how they are going to integrate more art this year, or how much they love second graders. That day, mixed in with the excitement and hope, teachers had a range of feelings—joy, skepticism, anger, apathy—and opinions about the reason they were spending seven hours a day for the next week learning about the new math texts and supplemental resources.

I sat among a group of three other teachers, all of us from the same school, which was known for its high poverty rate and low performance on standardized tests. We talked while sipping coffee and eating muffins. Ms. Wilson taught sixth grade, and this was to be her last year before retirement. She had a strong personality, and as a former union president, she was quick to invoke union-contract language, or just complain. "I have twenty-seven students and only ten boys," she said. "This is not going to be easy. Sixth-grade girls can be so nasty."

"I hear you have Jason," said Ms. Sherman. A fifth-grade teacher with five years' experience at our school, she was insecure about her teaching abilities and struggled with discipline in her class every year. "He just won't listen—he's out of his seat anytime you turn your head. He's always messing with the girls."

Ms. Harkins, another fifth-grade teacher with over twenty-five years' experience in mostly in affluent schools, strived to be positive about whatever the administration came up with. She had earned her principal credentials but had yet to get a job running a school. "I'm excited to use the science kits better this year. And this new math program should be great, too. Isn't this the one you piloted last year?" She was looking at me now.

"No, it was different, more like our old text in some ways—but with lots of problem-solving," I said. "I'm trying to be optimistic about this one, but I liked the program I piloted."

At that time, I had eight years of teaching experience. The previous year, I had been among a group of teachers who each piloted new math programs. The National Council of Teachers of Mathematics (NCTM) was establishing new standards for mathematics instruction—more communication, hands-on learning experiences, and problem-solving. I felt the program I had piloted demonstrated a healthy mix of procedures and concepts. I was a bit doubtful about the new math program we were all gathered to learn about but was trying to be open. "The next week will be interesting," I said.

"Why did the committee choose this one?" asked Ms. Wilson.

"They felt it was cutting-edge math." I chose my words carefully, trying not to get too snarky. "There were some very assertive folks on the committee who had the district coordinator's ear. I think there was some pressure put on, but I'm not sure."

"Well, I heard it was two principals who made a lot of noise about which program to choose because of what *their* teachers liked," said Ms. Wilson, who knew people in every school in the district. "Those schools are nothing like ours—they have no ELL students and virtually no poor families." (ELL refers to English language learners.)

Ms. Harkins, forever spinning positive, said, "I'm looking forward to it. I didn't have much success with the old program. I was supplementing it all the time."

Ms. Wilson seemed to ignore Ms. Harkins's comment and, with a certain edge to her voice that belied the hope of the new school year, said, "Every year it's something new." *Except your attitude,* I thought to myself. "Last year it was positive discipline. The year before that it was the new writing program, which turned out to be a mess, and the year before that, it was how to write a lesson plan, which was just stupid. This year it's this crazy math, and we're talking about a new reading program next year. The union is trying to put language in the contract that will limit the number of changes each year, but I don't think it will fly. And the school board is putting pressure on everyone. They are all so clueless about what happens in schools. All I know is I have to teach all subjects, and with this week of training and follow up-sessions, I don't have time to prepare for it at all."

I gazed off into the distance, dreaming of the golf I was not playing.

In another part of the gym, the publisher representative promoting the new mathematics text series was smiling and making small talk with teachers, trying to create a positive feeling about the week. A district administrator was also there to kick off the training and build enthusiasm. "I'm so happy to see all your smiling faces here for the start of a very important training on our new mathematics curriculum . . ."

Curriculum. This is a word that is often used with the assumption that everyone knows (and agrees on) what it means. This happens all the time in our daily lives. For example, in the United States we are fond of saying that we live in a democracy—where everyone has a say in how things work. However, we actually live in a representative republic, where we elect people to make decisions. Yet no one argues when politicians talk about democracy. In education, *curriculum* is a term thrown around in the same way. Typically, it is used in reference to textbooks; however, it means much more.

Curriculum is defined as: "All the courses of study offered by an educational institution" and "a group of related courses, often in a special field of study."[1] It comes from the Latin word *currere* meaning to run the course. I define curriculum as all the influences on a student's journey of education, some planned and organized, some not. I'm not alone in acknowledging all these influences, either; years ago, Washington State developed the SAILS model, which stands for standards, assessment, instruction and intervention, leadership, and system-wide commitment. SAILS is part of a comprehensive plan to improve literacy outcomes for all students.[2]

Below are what I see as the major elements of a student's curricular journey through education. Each is discussed in more detail in the chapters that follow.

Content: What's in the text? Content refers to textbooks, supplemental resources, and learning standards, which articulate what students should know and be able to do by the end of a certain grade.

Instruction: Who is teaching? How do teachers teach? How are they trained? Instruction includes the style of teaching and the methods used. Most educators agree that classroom teachers have the biggest influence on student achievement.

Assessment: How is learning measured? The kinds of assessments— formative, summative, chapter tests, standardized tests, et cetera—and how the results are used play a big role in what and how students learn.

Leadership: Who's guiding the educational journey and making the decisions? This group includes school board members, superintendents, curriculum directors, and other central office administrators, principals, vice principals, and teacher leaders like department heads.

Staff Development: How do we support our teachers in furthering their knowledge? It's important to consider not only what kind of continuing education teachers get and where they get it but also how open teachers are to training in the first place.

School Culture: How does it feel to be at a particular school? What are the prevailing attitudes, beliefs, and behaviors of students and staff? A school's culture can either make it easy or difficult for students to succeed and teachers to teach; the principal and staff are primarily the ones who establish the culture of a school.

Bias in School Culture

The way teachers interact with students can be telling about a school's culture. Once, I observed a teacher greeting new students in a biased fashion. For white students, the teacher was all smiles as he asked about their academic interests and where they might need help. The same teacher greeted Black students with a scowl, asking about learning and discipline problems and whether they had IEPs (individual education plans for special education).

Community Culture: How does the school relate to the surrounding community and vice versa? To what extent does the community value academics? Systemic issues in a community, such as racism and violence, infiltrate schools, affecting both students and teachers.

The better these elements of curriculum—content, instruction, assessment, leadership, staff development, school culture, and community culture—complement one another, the more effective and enjoyable a student's journey of learning will be. To address any one area in isolation discounts the other aspects of the education system. Ideally, decisions about school reform should consider *all* aspects of curriculum.

Journey to the Airport: Curriculum in Action

When I look back on my career in education, some of the most rewarding moments were when student learning came from experiences that extended lessons beyond the classroom, such as field trips. One field trip in particular stands out in my mind because of the way in which it opened up the world to students. It also demonstrates the interconnected nature of the elements of curriculum and how they can affect learning.

During the mid-1990s, the school where I worked was only a few miles from SeaTac International Airport. I often consulted with a friend who was a gifted teacher—learning from peers is a valuable form of staff development—and he gave me the idea of taking my sixth-grade students to SeaTac so they could interview passengers waiting for flights at the international terminal. (This was before 9/11, so airport security was much lighter then; you did not need a ticket to go to the gate area.)

The goal of the field trip was to help students build their oral and written communication skills and widen their perspective, to open up their world. (Many of the children had never ventured beyond their own neighborhoods.) Prior to the trip, I introduced students to the content: closed versus open-ended questions. Closed questions can be answered with a simple yes or no. For example, are you traveling for business? Open-ended questions require more in-depth answers: for example, what is the purpose of your trip? In class, students practiced asking each other open-ended questions and then recording the answers. Demonstrating good listening skills was a challenge for many. "That's not what I said!" was a comment I heard often at first.

To set up the field trip, I had to garner support from inside and outside the school. First, I had to reach out to the community; with one phone call, United Airlines gave me permission to bring the students to the gates at the south satellite of the airport—where many flights were departing for the Pacific Rim—to interview their customers. Community culture does not usually place a high value on education, but the company was pleased to be involved, recognizing the importance of education and supporting student learning experiences.

The culture of the school also played an important role in making the field trip possible. The principal, part of the school's leadership, trusted me and believed in my idea; she fostered an environment in which teachers' creative approaches to learning were generally well-received—and encouraged. (I often wonder if this would be the case now, in the era of test fever.) She gave me permission to take the field trip—as long as I didn't ask for money. The PTA was also pivotal in creating a school culture that supported teachers and students—there were about a dozen active families doing the bulk of the fund-raising and volunteering for the five-hundred-strong student body. Unfortunately, they could only afford to sponsor one field trip a year per classroom, so I couldn't ask them for funds. I had to figure out how to get my class the six miles from school to the airport on my own. School buses for trips like this aren't cheap—it would have cost about $150 to obtain one for a few hours. So, I decided to use public transportation instead. We would take a city bus.

Before I knew it, the day of the field trip arrived. "Make sure you have a couple of pens or pencils, your questions, and clipboards or pads of paper to write down answers from the people you talk to," I told the class. "You all know what kind of behavior I expect. As leaders of this school, you represent everyone here. So carry yourselves appropriately with the pride of knowing y'all are the best. Let's go to the bus stop."

When the bus pulled up, the driver's eyes got wide as he took in the crowd of twenty-eight students and three adults (myself and two parent volunteers) standing on the sidewalk, talking, giggling, and fidgeting. The children suddenly got quieter as they boarded. They beamed with excitement as they took their seats.

The kids chatted happily for the ten-minute ride to the bus center, where another bus would take us to the airport.

"Look, that's my house!"

"Oh, there's my mom going to work."

"Oh man, look at that car. That's cool!"

An interesting and amazing aspect of field trips is how students react to unfamiliar environments—I got to observe some surprising behavior shifts on this trip. For example, as we waited for the second bus, one group of boys, who tended to misbehave on the playground, were noticeably nervous. They grasped their clipboards and pencils tightly, looked all around, and shifted their weight back and forth as they huddled together only a couple of yards from me. Next to them was a group of girls who were often disruptive in class and tended to stir the pot. They appeared to be the most well-behaved and proper group of twelve-year-old girls you could imagine.

When we arrived at the airport, we moved together like a school of fish through the baggage claim area and onto the train that would take us to the terminal. Fellow passengers gave us curious looks—you just don't see a group of sixth graders with clipboards and pads of paper in the airport very often.

At the terminal, I said, "Remember to smile and look them in the eye. Everyone take a deep breath . . . Okay, go talk to folks."

Some students went right up to people and started their interviews. Others—a couple of the "tough" guys, the shyest girl in class, and two girls who were often involved in some sort of social drama—needed a little time to watch the others first, along with some prodding and encouragement from me. Shortly, every student was talking to adults at the two gates, except for one girl.

Abby was an uptight, dominant personality at school. A vocal child, she wore a frown most of the time and took out her frustrations on her classmates. Academically, she was a bit above average, with a real talent for writing, but she was also insecure and her friendships often had drama. She was afraid of looking or sounding "stupid." Sadly, she often called herself "ugly," though she had a bright smile and contagious laugh. Her aggressive behavior, as so often is the case, was a way to overcome her feelings of inadequacy.

"Mr. Green, what do I do if they don't want to talk to me? Are you sure we won't get in trouble? I don't want to do this." Her eyes darted around the room.

"Just stand here with me for now and watch the others. It's okay," I said. A long minute later. "What do think, Abby? You ready?"

"Mr. Green, I just don't think I can do this!"

"How about I go with you to your first interview? Let's talk to that nice woman over there." I pointed to a woman seated nearby with her hair in a bun. She had a look of amusement and interest on her face as she observed the other students performing their interviews. The woman was gracious, and in just a few moments, Abby was busy scribbling down answers and asking more questions.

Soon all students, including Abby, were talking to passengers en route to various destinations. The terminal was buzzing with chatter and smiles.

"Mr. Green, Mr. Green! I talked to that man by myself! He said he'll send me a card! I'm going to talk to that woman over there!" one of the students said. Part of the project also included asking the interviewees if they would send a postcard to the school from their destination.

Back in the classroom the next day, the students were excited to share their experiences of the interviews with the class. I assessed them on their ability to get more than one-word answers, to take good notes that they could later make sense of, and their class presentation. More important—though it can't be assigned a grade—was their glow of pride and sheer joy. It was obvious that conducting these interviews helped them build self-confidence, an essential quality to have in today's world. Abby was particularly proud that she had talked to twelve people when the requirement was only five to ten.

After about a week, we started receiving postcards from all over the world. The students then put them up on a map on the hallway bulletin board, catching the attention of anyone heading down the hall. Often students went out of their way to show the postcards to other students or adults.

I believe the field trip was a clear demonstration of how various elements of curriculum work together to create a positive learning experience. For one, the idea for the trip came from peer consultation—a staff development activity. The school and community cultures—and school leadership—all supported our efforts. The content goals were well-articulated. My approach to instruction included building trust: the students trusted I would keep them safe and provide them with unique opportunities to learn outside of a textbook; in turn, I trusted them to demonstrate maturity, responsibility, and respect. The students exceeded my expectations that day (not to mention those of other school staff members who, prior to the trip, had said things like, "You're taking them on the bus? With only two other adults? You're crazy"). As needed, I provided additional emotional support. Learning is easier when teachers demonstrate patience and understanding (yes, it seems obvious, but sometimes the students who need it the most don't always receive it). From time to time, we all need encouragement and to know that everything will be okay. The passengers were receptive to the children—an indicator of a community culture that values learning and curiosity. While some passengers were friendlier and more talkative than others, they were all polite and answered the questions posed to them. That was not surprising, as a wide-eyed eleven- or twelve-year-old obviously doing a school assignment is hard to resist. The number of postcards we later received did surprise me—people had to make a special effort to send those. Every student received at least one or two postcards, and a few received more. It was one of those moments when people, absolute strangers, showed humanity, rejuvenating my faith in the world.

How common is it for these elements of curriculum to consistently complement one another, resulting in meaningful learning experiences for students? I wish I could say it was often.

Looking at the Big Picture

Unfortunately, when adults start talking about school reform, it's hard for me to maintain the same sense of confidence and optimism I experienced during that field trip. But I have not lost all hope for an equitable education system—and neither should you. There are parents, educators, and other professionals out there working tirelessly to improve educational opportunities for disadvantaged children, navigate funding and resource gaps, and foster a love of learning that extends into adulthood—and some are even achieving success. But to bring about holistic, sustainable improvements, we have to start questioning the way we traditionally approach education.

For example, if teachers are required to have a clear goal for any lesson plan, or field trip, then why don't we have a clear unifying purpose for public schools? Why do we continue plodding along with the same basic parameters established long ago—age-based grade levels from kindergarten through twelfth grade, mid-afternoon dismissal, September through June school year, and results from once-a-year tests viewed as the ultimate measure of success or failure? As a society, we blow smoke about honoring innovation and creativity, yet in many schools, textbooks prescribe the pace at which teachers teach lessons, regardless of the skills and knowledge of the students (or if there was a bee in the classroom!). Why do we accept this?

We fool ourselves by thinking that everyone can succeed based on reaching rigorous standards, measured by annual tests. There are many other aspects—and inequities—that are part of education in the United States. Creating a public educational system that truly benefits all children will take a great shift in thinking. We need to reevaluate and articulate the beliefs that guide our actions.

In the chapters that follow, we will examine each aspect of curriculum to clarify its part in the bigger picture. I'll point out some of the problems as well as the positive aspects of, and the possibilities within, today's system. The complexity can be overwhelming, but our children—no matter what race, religion, gender, economic background, or sexual orientation—are worth the effort.

Chapter 2

Content: What Is Taught?

Follow the Script

How is the content of a particular subject area like mathematics or social studies chosen? Who chooses it? Each state sets guidelines for content that are based on that state's learning standards—the academic goals for each grade. For example, a learning standard might specify that a fourth-grade child can multiply two-digit by two-digit numbers accurately. School districts must then follow state guidelines when they select content. Each school district is also responsible for providing teachers with resources, such as textbooks, which supposedly teach to the state learning standards. Sounds simple, right? Yet this is where the situation becomes complicated. Textbook series all come with guidelines on best usage. What this means is that textbooks, and therefore textbook publishers, are often the ones guiding instruction— and the extent to which they dictate what content is taught, how it's taught, and when it's taught may surprise you.

Mathematics is one subject in which the text has guided instruction in more classrooms than not. The teacher's editions have instructions— scripts even—that are often followed with few changes:

Open your books to page 12. Look at the example problem.
[Note: See how they lined up the numbers and carried the 3 to
the tens place.] Now try problem number one: 23 x 17=_____.
Keep your numbers neatly placed on the paper. Did you all
get 391? Make sure you carried the 2 to the tens place before
multiplying again. Let's do one more as a group . . .

While some students get the procedures, many don't. But teachers move on anyway, leading to frustrated students and misunderstanding of mathematics. The textbook is often the only resource used and is followed page by page from the beginning as far as teachers can get.

Teachers' attitudes about how closely to follow mathematics textbooks can lead to stress. For example, when I took an eighth-grade mathematics teacher position in a middle school, I quickly found the teachers' attitudes toward the text were quite pronounced. In my first math department meeting at this school, with three other full-time math teachers, we discussed the upcoming year. Since I was new to the school, I was quiet, trying to get a feel for the group, but others jumped right in with their opinions.

Ms. Franke had been teaching middle school math for twenty-three years. With a sharp look to everyone and no one over her glasses, and a tone to match, she declared, "I have to be through six chapters by the end of December; otherwise, I won't get to the geometry in May."

Ms. Bowhart, who had been teaching at this middle school for the last sixteen years sat back in her chair (it was her room we met in) and nodded in agreement. "In algebra, we have to do 176 assignments, 16 chapter tests, and 4 unit tests in only 180 days, so I have to double up some assignments. The kids just need to keep up." Then she smiled at me, a smile I could not return.

I am sure I had a surprised look on my face—their take on teaching math was very different from mine. I had spent eleven years in elementary schools where teachers, of course, tried to follow the text but would often spend longer on lessons than the book called for if they believed students needed more time. I didn't always follow the order of the chapters, either. For example, I would often skip the review of addition and subtraction and jump to fractions, where students would use addition, subtraction, multiplication, and division in a different way. Having the book dictate what teachers do seems to forget that students are individuals who each learn at their own pace.

Some teachers are creative and bring in other resources or use other methods to teach the same content, but most just use whatever the district or school provides. While I was student teaching, one veteran fifteen-year teacher said, "My job is to teach with what they give me, not create curriculum." I can understand the thinking, yet I was one who looked for other resources to make learning more accessible to students. For example, my students "played" the stock market to learn about decimals, fractions, and percentages rather than just doing a page of calculations.

Many of the textbook series for elementary schools are now even more scripted, with strict guidelines for sequencing concepts, maintaining a certain pace, and following routines like, for example, dictating when to work in groups or individually, or how to handle homework. There are some schools that *require* teachers to teach certain lessons according to the timetable in the textbook, not according to when the children actually learn the concepts. Otherwise, students would not get through the planned materials and required learning and would therefore be behind the following year. Some principals hover to ensure teachers keep up. As a result, some teachers spend less time on other subjects, like social studies and art, if their students need more time to comprehend the material. Mathematics has been considered a key subject in the United States for many decades, and textbooks have evolved during this time. Yet it is an area where many people struggle throughout their lives, including elementary teachers who teach *all* subjects.

Teachers may rely on the textbooks because they feel they have to or because they do not feel confident in their own mathematics knowledge. No matter what the reason, it is a disservice to the students (and insulting to the teachers who do understand mathematics). When teachers rely solely on textbooks, children get exposed only to what the publishers of the textbook deem necessary; teachers are supposed to follow the guidelines and scripts provided (the publisher's way of ensuring that any teacher can teach the content). It's hard to teach to the individual that way. Yet new textbooks are touted as a solution to low math test scores and subpar achievement, if followed with fidelity. "Just trust the program" was what one publisher representative told me once when I questioned how a particular text series fostered necessary skills. But why adopt a new mathematics text series in the first place? Mathematics, especially elementary mathematics, hasn't changed . . . or has it?

Mathematics: What's the Big Deal?

Mathematics, along with science, has been a subject area of emphasis in school improvement efforts for decades. A big push came in 1957, in the heat of the Cold War, when the Soviet Union put a man into space before the United States. There was quite the outcry about how and why that could happen. After his election in 1960, President Kennedy challenged the country to put a man on the moon before the Soviets. Policy makers and administrators scrambled to formulate a plan to achieve this. Hoping to inspire more rocket scientists, literally, they turned to public schools and examined how math and science were being taught. They outfitted classrooms with more technology and lab kits, and they decided that teaching practices needed to change—hence New Math was born.

New Math generated much controversy. Elementary mathematics became more than just doing arithmetic or crunching numbers. There was an effort to teach students mathematical concepts through the introduction of set theory and numbers not in base ten.

What Is Base Ten?

Base ten is our traditional decimal system. Within this system, the number twelve means two ones and one group of ten. But, for example, in another decimal system such as base five, the number twelve means two ones and one group of five. Thus, twelve in base five equals seven in our traditional base ten decimal system. If you're shaking your head in confusion, you're not alone.

In New Math, elementary students were taught different numeral systems like binary numbers, used in computer technology. There was more use of materials, like beans, for students to manipulate, to enhance their understanding of sets (groups). Many educators felt it was too abstract; implementation of New Math was a mix of dysfunction and total success. Though New Math did not last more than a few years, due to lots of disagreement and parental frustrations, it was an attempt at improving student achievement. The goal of getting students to understand the concepts behind the procedures of mathematics was to make algebra and other higher math more accessible.

Textbook series and instructional practices in mathematics have been evolving ever since. The balance of conceptual understanding and procedural instruction in mathematics continues to be a major issue. Some people feel learning mathematics is about solving a page of equations, while others think it's about applying mathematics to stories or situations—like construction estimates. I believe being able to understand why you are adding, subtracting, multiplying, or dividing numbers is important, as well as being able to actually do the number crunching. (Or at least be able to estimate, so you know if you multiplied by 200 instead of 2,000 on the calculator.)

Another important landmark in the evolution of mathematics instruction came in the early 1980s during the Reagan administration with the publishing of "A Nation at Risk." The report, published by the US Department of Education (which Reagan had previously wanted to abolish), lambasted US schools as wallowing in mediocrity that could seriously damage the quality of life in this country. The job landscape was shifting more rapidly than ever to white-collar jobs, requiring different knowledge and skills than blue-collar work. In order to stay competitive in the increasing technological economy, the report called for change that gave young people the education necessary to find work. In response, publishers again put forth new textbook series and instructional programs, trying to find the best way to teach mathematics.

Yet nearly sixty years after the space race, and over thirty years after Reagan, we still have issues with public school student achievement in mathematics and science. In 2017, for example, only 40 percent of fourth graders and 34 percent of eighth graders achieved a proficient level in mathematics on the National Assessment of Educational Progress, an assessment that is often dubbed the "nation's report card."[3]

The media regularly reports on low test scores and how US students lag behind their international counterparts in mathematics and science instruction. While the Trends in International Mathematics and Science Study—a commonly cited test for judging student achievement nationwide compared to other countries—reports improvements in test scores, the results are still below what is expected. In 2015, US eighth graders ranked tenth out of over forty countries,[4] which is better than fifteenth in 2003 or nineteenth in 1999. But the results are still below countries like Japan, Kazakhstan, and Canada. Not cool since we are "supposed" to be the best in the world at everything.

Mathematics instructional methods and content have been areas of focus at the state level as well. In Washington, higher standards and accountability in mathematics for high school graduation have been emphasized, especially since 2000. With about half of Washington State college freshmen requiring remedial mathematics courses (nationwide about one-third of college freshmen need remedial mathematics), the need for improved K–12 mathematics instruction seems obvious. For better and for worse, the method most often employed to improve mathematics instruction, and therefore test scores, is to adopt a new text series.

Implementation: Easier Said Than Done

Most of the schools where I worked had test results that were usually lower than state averages, though similar in some years. Thus, I experienced several new text series adoptions—administrations' efforts to improve those results, especially in mathematics. Elementary and middle school mathematics do provide the foundation for all mathematics, so a new text series that's touted to improve student achievement at all levels makes sense to a lot of people. But implementing a new text series is often a challenge.

For one thing, there is no uniformity to how often districts make wholesale changes of this magnitude. Some will adopt a new text series every seven years, while others adopt new texts only when they have funding or as a reaction to poor test scores. Often what is not taken into account is that it takes anywhere from *three* to *seven years* for new instructional resources to be fully implemented and to demonstrate efficacy (or not). One reason is that the progression of each curriculum from grade to grade is unique. Starting in kindergarten and continuing on through each grade level, children must gradually master the skills and build the vocabulary necessary for successfully learning the content at each grade level.

However, districts adopt elementary programs for all grades at once, mostly for budgetary reasons. Teachers are often trying to fill in years of required background knowledge before they can start on the day's lesson. That can be frustrating to teachers, and students. Some teachers go to great lengths to meet individual student needs, some students get extra help outside the classroom, and some teachers just go on with the lessons, whether students have mastered the background knowledge or not. Consider that a fifth-grade teacher has to wait six years for a group of students to have all the prerequisite experiences necessary before he or she can assess whether those students have achieved the goals touted by the publisher.

Patience is necessary, though typically absent in these days of immediate gratification. Test scores, new tests that evaluate student ability, media pressure, or turnover of school administration can all influence whether a certain resource like a textbook series is given the required time to demonstrate efficacy. Lack of patience just adds stress and doesn't help students learn more.

Another challenge to implementing a new text series is teachers' attitudes. Often there is a general mistrust of anything the district administration comes up with. Many teachers feel that administrators are too far removed from classrooms and have no real sense of how their decisions actually affect the teachers themselves and their students. Also, let's face it—some adults just do not like being told what to do.

Staff room conversations can be very telling about teacher reactions to district-wide changes, such as new texts. For example, one day, during a break in one of the trainings for a new mathematics text series that was being adopted, I went to the staff room to sit in an adult chair (third-grade desks just don't fit me well at all) and get a cup of coffee. My colleagues, who had assertive personalities and really did care about their students, were sharing their opinions freely about the new textbooks.

"I still don't see why we need new math texts," Ms. Wilkes snapped, a second-grade teacher with twelve years' experience. "I liked the ones we had."

Here we go again, I thought, *more complaining.* I didn't say a word, thinking I would make the most of the teaching tools I was given. Besides, whether I liked it or not, I couldn't change the district directive.

Ms. Larson, a twenty-year veteran fourth-grade teacher, waved her hands in the air as she spoke. "Just because some administrator, who hasn't been in the classroom for years, thinks it will help our test scores, we have to spend all this time in workshops trying to figure out this new program. I have other things to teach!"

"My kids can't read and all this problem-solving is about reading, not math," added Ms. Jansen, a third-grade teacher with twenty-two years in the same classroom.

"It doesn't have enough skill practice. I'll have to use my old worksheets," Ms. Wilkes said. "More time wasted at the copy machine—*if* it's working!"

While I understood their frustration, and in some cases even shared it, I was just trying to relax and they were not helping.

Ms. Larson asserted, with a bit of an attitude, "We spend weeks on test prep anyway. This won't help."

Then they all chimed in at once. "It's all about the test!"

The increased pressure surrounding test scores, especially in reading and mathematics, is something most teachers I worked with resented and felt was not conducive to learning. There is more to learning than test scores, but that seems to be the purpose of public schools to many. Some teachers welcome new materials like textbooks, but more often than not, they see the adoption of new textbooks as top-down directives from those who don't spend much time in classrooms. And children are savvy listeners—they pick up on their teachers' skepticism. What student is motivated to learn when their teacher is subtly, or not so subtly, scoffing at the material? After all, many teachers feel they are the best judges of what their students need to learn and what is necessary to make that happen. Whether such knowledge and skills coincide with established learning standards is another issue.

Learning Standards: A Good Idea But . . .

What is it all about? What are the goals of kindergarten through high school education? I have heard many teachers emphatically say, "I know what my students need to know." Yet if we are serious about educating all children, we need more concrete, consistent guidelines.

No matter what they are labeled—standards, learning objectives, or essential learning requirements—the goals for each grade and subject have been around for several decades. When I started teaching in Washington State, there was some variance between district requirements. This was part of why the essential academic learning requirements were established in core subjects like reading and mathematics. One goal of standardizing was to ensure that students across the state could learn and acquire the same basic skills and knowledge no matter what schools they attended. Until late 2016, most of the US was collaborating on establishing and implementing the Common Core State Standards. Politics have influenced a movement away from Common Core, but standards and goals for students in some form will endure.

As of the publication of this book, Common Core standards exist in the areas of English language arts and mathematics. The purpose is to articulate clearly what students are expected to learn in order to be successful in college and careers. Consistency in core subjects among schools, districts, and states gives children a better chance at a coherent educational experience.

One of the reasons adopting Common Core standards is important is the high mobility of students during the school year—children who change schools when their families move (which happens often, especially for students in poverty). For example, in Seattle Public Schools, most schools have between a 4 percent and 50 percent mobility rate.[5] When I was teaching, my students' mobility rate was usually between 10 percent and 40 percent, meaning that a class of thirty students at the beginning of the year could have anywhere between three to ten different students by June.

While adopting subject standards improves consistency for students, especially in mathematics and reading, there are other elements, often overlooked, that are just as important for achieving academic success—even the Common Core State Standards Initiative website acknowledges that. Below are just a few of the complications of overreliance on learning standards.

First of all, standards, so far at least, exist only in the areas of reading and mathematics. There is a lot more to a quality education than those two subjects, though test results in mathematics and reading are used predominately in judging schools' effectiveness. Even so, if and when other subject area standards are developed, life is not segregated into neat subject areas. Many elementary school teachers *do* integrate content areas because they teach all subjects, and are even encouraged by administration to do so. However, in middle and high schools, the connections that abound between subjects like social studies, language arts, mathematics, and the sciences are rarely fostered or even acknowledged.

For example, a seventh-grade mathematics teacher can be so focused on planning and teaching 150 students in five classes—grading papers, attending department meetings, going to staff meetings, and, of course, serving on various committee meetings—that it is easy to focus only on the textbook and care only about what students are doing in that one class. Thus any possible connections across content areas are usually not made. Yet it doesn't take much to point out the importance of accurate graphs used in social studies, how equations are used in estimating materials necessary for building a bookshelf, how sheet music uses fractions, or how reading comprehension is vital to accurate problem-solving.

This is one facet of education that confuses and frustrates a lot of middle and high school students. Each hour is fragmented and detached from the next. Throughout my career, I heard many students say—and I remember the feeling myself when I was a student—that each teacher was so focused on teaching their content area and giving assignments unrelated to other schoolwork that each subject felt isolated in a way that just didn't make sense. It became easy for students to not try in subject areas that didn't particularly interest them (especially if they didn't like or respect the teacher).

Individual lessons and skills make more sense when students can see the mathematics in art, nature, and their environment or realize that understanding an author's purpose in a story can help them be better critical thinkers and consumers. While there are schools that do create learning experiences across content areas (actually, a lot of gifted programs do this), it is not the norm. Some middle and high schools make an attempt at collaboration by scheduling meetings between teachers from different subject areas, with varying degrees of successful implementation. In my experience, the general idea was well-received by teachers, but the details became too much. The amount of time necessary for planning just wasn't there for effective coordination. There was also little guidance from administrators. In reality, everyone just left the meetings and did their own thing.

As an eighth-grade math teacher, my solution to this problem was to give extra credit to students who could show how math skills could be used in other classes, such as shop, science, music, and social studies. For example, some students realized they were using math to determine the cost of materials for sewing a quilt. Others discovered how fractions were used in music to show the value of notes or beats per measure, or how graphs and charts in social studies depicted trends in immigration. It helped a few students see how subjects are connected and reinforced the content without my having to convince other teachers to coordinate with me.

Aside from the single-minded focus of learning standards, another issue is that important life skills that are not subject specific are absent from the standards; for example, how to collaborate productively (particularly with someone you don't like) and complete a task, how to ask questions relevant to solving a problem, how to take initiative, how to apply prior knowledge to new situations, and how to remain open to new learning. People just assume students develop those skills in school, and while some students do learn and use them, more could be successful if they were explicitly taught and encouraged to develop those habits.

While there are many schools and teachers that are dedicated to interdisciplinary connections and the explicit teaching of the life skills mentioned above, many decision-makers perceive it as a distraction from improving test scores in reading and math. Some people don't realize that test scores will improve with the development of skills that help students think and problem-solve, no matter what the situation.

Life Skills Lessons

There are programs that teach these skills, such as the Advancement Via Individual Determination or project-based learning. Yet they are not common and many students don't have access to them—or the programs get cut when new administration comes in. In the absence of these programs, students may miss out on lessons that teach life skills, especially if their parents didn't do well in school and don't have the ability to teach them.

It is important to have clear goals for learning. A vision for what students should know and be able to do allows educators to focus their lessons. All students, no matter how much money their parents make or where they live, should receive high-quality education with clear expectations that will help them become productive citizens. Deciding what those goals are and how they should be reached is where complications occur over the different methods.

A Little Imagination Goes a Long Way

While it's important to teach lessons that address learning standards—however flawed the concept of standards may be—teachers can make lessons fun and meaningful, increasing the odds that students will engage thoughtfully with the content. There is a place for some practice of individual skills, like being able to add, subtract, multiply, and divide whole numbers, decimals, and fractions, but it is the application in different situations that makes learning meaningful. Robert Moses, civil rights activist and mathematics professor, created his Algebra Project with that in mind. He observed that many students, especially students of color and in poverty, did not get beyond algebra, which is the gateway to higher mathematics and a prerequisite for admission to universities. Since traditional algebra was too abstract for many students to understand, the premise of his program was presenting situations that students could relate to, and then showing how algebra was germane to those situations. For example, he explored how traveling to a location, with landmarks along the way, could be described using positive and negative numbers. The point was to create engaging, pertinent ways of teaching the standards, not found in most textbooks.

What follows are examples of projects that incorporated various content areas and taught life skills, presented via lessons in meaningful and compelling ways to students. The ideas for these projects did not come from any textbook. Most were inspired by other teachers or personal experiences. My philosophy was that if I thought the content was boring or mundane, then undoubtedly the students would, too. My point in sharing these examples is to show that it is possible to teach content in a way that addresses learning standards while engaging students' curiosity and hopefully a passion for life. Can you imagine the possibilities if school reform efforts focused less on testing and following textbook protocols and focused more on helping teachers find relevant ways to naturally engage students' curiosity?

Currency and Cruising the Globe

During my first year as a certified teacher, I was a long-term substitute for a sixth-grade class. I had accumulated a collection of coins and some paper currency from several European countries I had visited during my studies at a German university. While working with decimals in mathematics, I used the money to bring a little something different to the exercises. For example, I asked the students to calculate what a loaf of bread, which cost $3.50 here in the US, would cost in lira (one dollar being worth 1,950 lira). Or how many nights a tourist could afford to stay at a Seattle hotel with 1,000 Norwegian kroner (this was before the euro). The students enjoyed looking at the various coins, holding them, and realizing that just because a coin had a large number on it didn't mean it was worth a lot. The beauty of a 500-lira coin is still palpable to me, though it was worth only about a quarter.

At the same time the students were learning about decimals in math, the social studies curriculum focused on South America and Canada. I wanted to engage students in what life was really like on those continents, not just review the boring textbook information. It was during a conversation with the librarian, who knew I liked to give creative assignments that integrated library resources and research skills, wherein she suggested the students write about what it would be like to travel to those places. So I assigned the students the task of writing an imaginary ten-day travel diary. (The first couple of years I had them choose only from South America or Canada, but then I opened it up to wherever they wanted to "visit." Why squash motivated, intellectual inquiry?)

The task of imagining what ten days would be like in a foreign country was daunting for some students (even those who regularly visited relatives elsewhere), yet everyone was motivated. In their diary entries, students had to use exchange rate information to track spending in their hundred-dollar-a-day budget. For example, they had to account for food, lodging, and recreational activities, among other things. Their diary entries also had to include enough activities to fill each day, though I allowed one day of resting by the pool. The librarian and I helped the students do research and come up with ideas for fun, affordable activities while traveling—I enjoyed the opportunity to learn about different countries myself. (Research was easier once I got internet access in my class in the mid-1990s.)

In their diaries, students also had to write down general information about the country, including details about language, art, the education system, government, history, cultural traditions, and other topics. Students had a few weeks to research and create their diaries. I allowed quite a bit of time to work on them in class, since a lot of students' home environments were not conducive to doing work. Also, I was able to check in, motivate, and provide help when needed.

The academic exercise of creative writing based on research allowed students to apply individual skills such as summarizing information, writing complete sentences and paragraphs, along with the math mentioned above—all while learning other important study and work habits, like following guidelines for a big project with many areas to cover, obtaining information from multiple sources, planning ahead to meet deadlines, persevering to complete a task, and showing creativity.

The travel diary project was a successful activity for assessing skills across multiple subject areas, but most importantly, it opened up the world to students. Years after one student completed his diary, he told me that this sixth-grade project inspired him to travel abroad. While he never went to Brazil, his travel diary destination, he lived and worked in South Africa, Greece, and China, while also traveling to other countries. Other former students also teach overseas now.

Children, young and old, have a natural curiosity that can motivate learning. The enthusiasm I had for learning about other places in the world and the hands-on effect of holding foreign money helped foster that curiosity and motivation while addressing learning standards and teaching some life skills. In addition, they began to see that there's a big world out there and the more they learn about it, the more choices open up to them, the more possibilities they can envision for their futures.

Maps and Blueprints

"I've never been to the beach at that park," one of my students exclaimed.

I was teaching at an elementary school — different from the one in the preceding section but in the same district — about one mile from a waterfront park and beach on Puget Sound. It was a park that, despite its close vicinity, about half of my class had not yet visited. Since the sound is so vital to life here in the Seattle area and outdoor education was a big part of sixth grade, I wanted to take the students to the shore for some investigating. We had no budget for field trips, but we were so close to the beach I decided we would walk there. I recruited a couple of adults to go with us, but it wasn't necessary really. As usual, once off school property, the students behaved well. Most of them were wide-eyed, especially after crossing a main road that was the unofficial border for many in the group.

Once at the park, the task was to create a cross-section map of the kinds of materials found on the beach, from the waterline all the way to about twenty yards inland. In pairs, students gathered small samples of sand, shells, pieces of wood, or whatever else they found and glued them to a piece of tagboard. The cross section would then show the elevation rise and how the beach changes as you get farther away from the water. Once they started looking carefully, the students noticed differences in the color and size of the sand and rocks. Several students commented on how many bread bag twist ties and small pieces of plastic there were. Seeing the effects of trash can bring home how important it is to keep our environment clean. Their powers of observation, an important skill for science, grew as they focused on their tasks. For example, some students noticed the intricate swirling patterns in the sand, indicating how the tide moved. The students not only learned a little more about our environment but also seemed to enjoy being able to move freely and breathe in the fresh sea air.

Similar to how the cross-section map was useful for teaching kids how to apply scientific skills, I used blueprints for students working with fractions—the bane of many a math student and teacher. Using a tape measure to create a floor plan to scale was a meaningful way to get students measuring and then mapping. We used the scale of a quarter inch equals one foot, just as in real blueprints. Students used graph paper to complete this project, and they had to be accurate and careful. Several students had to do a lot of erasing, as they got careless and would, for example, make a desk that actually measured two and a half feet by one and a half feet look like a one-foot square desk on paper (go ahead and use your ruler/tape measure to realize how small a desk that would be) or they'd completely leave out the front door.

That exercise was the warm-up for then creating an apartment floor plan. I first asked them to do some measuring at their homes to see how big certain features were, like kitchen counters, hallways, and closets, for example. Then I gave them a thousand square feet to create an apartment they wanted. This was not an easy task because students had to keep track of square footage and meet certain building code requirements, such as three-foot-wide doors.

The next step was to design a house. Everyone got a certain size lot within a neighborhood and a list of requirements for the house and property, like not building within ten feet of property lines. I allowed hot tubs but no swimming pools, as that was just too far-fetched economically. We then created our neighborhood. This required some compromise and negotiation among the students:

"I don't want to look into your bedroom—can't you put it on the other side?" one asked.

"You should put a hedge there and look out the other way."

One year we even got to the point of making scale models of the homes out of cardboard. Students had to figure out how much carpet and paint they would need. The various levels of this blueprint exercise gave them an opportunity to not only practice using our measurement system in an imaginative way but also see how fractions were relevant to their everyday lives. The students got a lot of practice calculating with fractions—as much as, if not more than, if I had assigned them worksheets or a textbook problem set.

Playing the Stock Market

Another activity that I frequently used to help teach computational skills, like converting fractions to decimals, was playing the stock market. Stock listings at the time used one-eighth of dollar increments to report stock value. Students had $100,000 to invest, and we would track their stocks' progress for several months. Not only is it fun to pretend you have $100,000 to invest and to keep track of your gains and losses, but working with decimals and fractions in this way is a lot more interesting than just doing a page of number-crunching problems. I found the students retained computational skills more easily because they were using them in a context they could relate to. To enhance the connection to current events, I encouraged students to pay attention to news stories we read about in class and how they seemed to affect certain stocks.

Once I got help from a parent who was in the early stages of starting a financial advising business. He volunteered to talk to the students about how stocks and investments worked, stressing the importance of long-term investing—ten years minimum. He was great with the students, and his presentation helped them understand the influences of the market better. Afterward, we started "charging" the students a 1 percent commission on every transaction for a more realistic experience. The students liked the activity and would get excited about sharing their portfolios with each other.

Though a majority of my students' families couldn't imagine having investment capital, it opened up the idea of investing and long-term financial planning for the students, which could benefit them years later. One girl got so excited about investing that she took her savings of a hundred dollars to buy a share of stock. It was thrilling to prompt an eleven-year-old girl to forgo the instant gratification that our society tends to promote and instead think about the future.

Luckily, I had principals who mostly supported efforts like this to create meaningful and engaging lessons. In schools where behavior issues often dominated classrooms, I was able to avoid a lot of it by just creating different lessons. The students knew we were doing activities not found in the textbooks (part of the benefit of teaching students who had been in school a few years and knew my reputation for creating interesting activities), and most of them really got into the work. Learning about the world while building the desired academic skills is certainly beneficial to students—and possible with a little imagination.

Ethnic-Specific Literature

Reading is another key content area where textbooks and scripted lessons may not engage the learner. Like many teachers, I used novels for reading instruction. Good literature offers another way to bring truth and ideas into the classroom. It is easier for readers to learn something from a story if they can relate to the settings and characters authentically, especially a reluctant reader. Who the author is also matters, especially to children of color and poverty. Stories of white middle-class, suburban life do not mean much to an immigrant child living in Section 8 housing.

Ethnic-specific literature refers to stories in which the author has the same ethnicity as the main characters. This is important because students can sense when a book is written by someone who knows what they are talking about versus an outsider (often a white male point of view). But the ethnic-specific nature of a story was only one of the criteria that I looked for when introducing novels to my class. The stories also had to be engaging, with themes related to family, friendship, and honesty, as in values that transcend cultures and do not reinforce negative stereotypes. The stories we read had to be authentic depictions of the cultures they represented, and of course I had to have read them. (I actually enjoy children's books.)

Authors such as Sandra Cisneros, Gary Soto, Walter Dean Myers, Mildred Taylor, Laurence Yep, Yoshiko Uchida, Belle Yang, and Kenneth Thomasma have written great stories that deal honestly with racism and prejudice, as well as themes of community, love, and respect. We did read books by white authors as well, but stories about a ten-year-old's experience being sent to Japanese internment camps or about a twelve-year-old boy's modern life in Harlem offer perspectives that we all should be aware of.

Children can sense honesty (even if they can't necessarily articulate it), and the authenticity of the stories made it easy for us to discuss what it means to be a friend, to be responsible, and deal with frustration because the situations were relatable to all my students, even the white ones. Once, while guest teaching in a fifth-grade class, we read a story about a young Chinese girl and her family (*Hannah Is My Name* by Belle Yang). Fearful of deportation, the family was waiting anxiously for their green cards. During our group discussion about the book, a young Hispanic boy said, "I thought only Mexicans had to get green cards." Not only did he learn that several of his classmates had or were hoping for green cards, but we also had a great discussion about immigration laws.

This experience points to the positive benefits of using different materials to teach skills such as reading comprehension, building vocabulary, empathizing with characters from different backgrounds, and understanding how a country's laws affect individuals, families, and entire populations. The more students can understand about the way our society functions outside of school, the better chance they have of finding their niche and also maybe discovering where they can make a positive impact within their communities.

Connecting to Life Outside the Neighborhood

The newspaper was a treasure trove of material for learning. Even though newspapers were more of a common source of information in the 1980s and '90s than now, due to technology, they still have lots of material appropriate for instruction, especially in the middle grades. Every Wednesday a set of local papers was delivered and used regularly for various activities. There was always some item of interest or controversy. We would read about environmental issues like water quality as well as even more controversial issues such as the use of the N-word in rap music and on the street. Reading strategies such as determining an author's purpose from editorials, connecting the newspaper content to other materials—like previous newspaper articles or social studies texts—and using context clues to help with vocabulary were easily integrated. The level of reading comprehension was appropriate, challenging, and the side effect of learning about the world was rewarding. Students definitely had their eyes opened to life beyond their neighborhood. (I enjoyed when students would question how things had gotten so "messed up.")

Sometimes emotions would be stirred by items in the news. Reading about the atrocities in the war in Kosovo in 1999, especially the stories of children left homeless or injured by the violence, hit us all hard. The class wanted to do something to help. After some discussion, we decided to raise money for Mercy Corps, a nonprofit organization cited in the newspaper as one of the more effective charities. Since the school barbecue was upcoming, we decided to hold a bake sale that day (with principal approval). Over half of my students' families relied on government assistance—I was struck by their generosity and their desire to help other children who were in dire need, even children halfway across the world. My students took on the responsibility of organizing the event, from getting permission from the principal to procuring items for sale, to selling the baked goods and counting all the money. We raised over $240 in one day! The students were so proud and felt appreciated when we got a letter from Mercy Corps thanking them. I, of course, was and am very proud and impressed by what they did.

By reading about current events, my students were able to connect to the larger world, while still learning skills articulated in the standards. When people are motivated to act for the benefit of others, we are all better off.

"When I'm an Adult . . ."

"Man, when I get out of school, I'm going to buy a new car, live in a nice place, one with a pool."

"I want a big house with a big yard and a three-car garage."

I overheard these kinds of comments from my students all the time. It is normal for young people to imagine their lives as adults; however, I thought it would help them value school more if they could see how important an education was to choosing the adult lifestyle they wanted.

Using the newspaper again as a resource, we looked for jobs in the classified section (before this content could be found online). The students then wrote letters (practicing business-letter writing) to employers, informing them who they were and asking about job prerequisites, in particular education and work experience. They also asked for an application. The students received many responses. They found out firsthand that the good-paying jobs they were interested in required more than a high school education and some significant work experience.

This assignment led to discussions about other kinds of education besides college, like apprenticeships or specialized programs such as cosmetology. We talked about what it meant to earn a living wage. Again using the newspaper, the students looked for housing in the classifieds section and grocery shopped using the food ads and coupons for pricing guides. We discussed utility costs, transportation ("I'll just take the bus like my mom. Cars are expensive"), insurance, and how the cost of living adds up quickly. While practicing reading, writing, and math skills, students could see for themselves (a much more valuable, lasting lesson than just being *told*) how education can lead to better opportunities in life—practical information not found in any textbooks that I'm aware of.

While many of the projects and experiences I have described in this chapter would be much harder to pull off today, because of the increase in test fever, these kinds of activities benefit all students as they try to make sense of the world and figure out where they fit within it. Reading and mathematics test scores would benefit from opportunities to apply skills in various situations not found in textbooks. That is something that seems to be discouraged in general education, though encouraged in gifted education, which isn't right. *Everyone* deserves high-quality educational experiences.

The content of curriculum, or what is taught, is supposed to be articulated in standards yet often is led by textbooks. How teachers regard and use the text can affect how much students are able to learn.

With learning standards in mind, creative experiences, like the examples I've provided throughout this chapter, can provide valuable learning opportunities, not based on a textbook, that engage children's natural sense of curiosity and open their eyes to the diversity of the world. As you will see in the next chapter, no matter what resource is used or what the goal of the lesson or unit is, it is the teacher's instruction that has the biggest impact on student achievement.

Chapter 3

Instruction: Who Teaches and How Do They Teach?

Math Class, Two Ways

Picture a group of twenty-eight ten- and eleven-year-old fifth graders squirming in their seats, trying to find their math text and homework. The students' desks are in straight rows, while the teacher is barricaded in the front of the room behind a stack of books on a five-foot-long table. She stands next to the overhead projector, fumbling with a pile of worksheets. The room is full of teetering piles of books, folders overflowing with papers, and stacks of boxes with labels like "Xmas," "Poetry," and "Soc. Studies." There is a cramped, chaotic feeling that something or someone is going to crash or implode at any moment. The whiteboard behind the teacher is full of information: the daily schedule, a list of students with missing work, names of students and their assigned classroom jobs, and a jumble of other miscellaneous information. Next to the whiteboard is a poster of an orange tabby cat hanging from a metal bar with its front paws. Beneath the cat it says, "Hang in there, baby!"

The teacher pulls down the projector screen. "All right now, quiet down so we can check yesterday's work." Her voice sounds strained as she tries to be heard over the half-dozen conversations among the students. After lobbing several verbal reprimands, adding names of misbehaving students to the board, and giving dirty looks to repeat offenders, the teacher asks for the answer to the first math problem.

Several hands shoot up; a couple of voices blurt out answers. The teacher calls on a girl in the front row who gives the correct answer. She is quickly rewarded with a Jolly Rancher hard candy.

"Who has the answer to number 2?" the teacher asks.

Amid a soft din of rustling papers and grumbling voices, another girl near the teacher gives a correct answer and receives a Jolly Rancher reward. This call-and-response goes on for about twenty-five minutes, with interruptions for explaining answers and reprimanding students: "Where is your work?" "Why isn't your book open?" "Shhhh!" "What have you been doing the last ten minutes?"

Another twenty minutes pass. By now, most of the students have consumed at least two hard candies and whatever other snacks they have stashed in their desks. The teacher—striving to be heard over the dull roar of students talking, shuffling pages and papers, and scooting their chairs—demonstrates the day's math lesson. She emphasizes just copying the steps of her solution, with no explanation as to why or how she knew what to do. Once the teacher is finished with the lesson, she sits down at her desk. The surrounding stacks of papers and books, as well as her computer, create a U-shaped enclosure accessible only from a side "alley." A line of about six students awkwardly holding books and notebooks snakes into this alley, waiting for help to complete the assignment just given. The hum of voices in the room adds to the atmosphere of borderline chaos, confusion, apathy, and boredom.

Later that day in the room next door, another fifth-grade class is learning the same lesson in mathematics. As you walk in the room, you immediately sense the culture encourages thinking and is centered on the children. There is a couch with cushions on one side of the room, with a couple of big cushions on the area rug also. There are several bookshelves full of children's literature, organized like a library. Student art is all over the room. Several displays of student projects are neatly arranged on the back table. The feel of a positive learning community fills the air.

The class has a quiet hum of pencils on paper and whispering voices. There are six groups of four children and one group of five all working in pods on the mathematics assignment. At each table group are bins with rulers, calculators, markers, bags of plastic circles and squares that have various numbers of equal-sized pieces (for fractions), and a few other tools. A few of the groups are using materials and one or two calculators are out, though used sparingly.

The teacher is sitting at one of the table groups, asking questions like "How did you know whether to multiply or divide?" and "Can you show me where that data came from?" or "Be ready to show your solution to the class later—it shows great understanding!"

Over the next twenty-five minutes, the teacher sits with each table group, asks questions, and gives some explanations, though mostly encourages other students to answer classmates' questions. A few times she reminds the class that they will be sharing their work at eleven o'clock and to be ready. She does have to ask two groups to talk a little quieter as the time for sharing approaches.

At eleven, each group of students takes turns sharing their work in front of the class. The other students sit quietly and listen, albeit they are a bit squirmy. One of the presenters asks if there are any questions. A couple of hands shoot up. One girl is called on. "Why did you divide by three? I don't see that in the problem." Another student says, "I don't see how you checked your work. How do you know you're right?"

After a couple more questions, the next group gets up and shares their work and answers questions. The teacher says very little during this time. When she does offer praise and helpful feedback, it is directly tied to concrete aspects of the students' work. "Your diagram of the problem is well-labeled and organized so that we can see your steps." "Would it help if you had added pictures?" "Remember to make the reasons *why* you did certain steps clearer, not just say, 'We added here.'" "Your group organized the workload so that each person was responsible for an equal part of the assignment."

After each group has presented their work, the teacher spends about fifteen minutes explaining the day's lesson. There are a few questions before the groups assemble again to start on the new assignment.

Enthusiasm for understanding and learning, as well as a sense of calm, permeates the atmosphere in this room.

Both teachers in these examples attended the same trainings for using the new mathematics program. They both have significant experience teaching, seven and twelve years, respectively. The difference between what happens in neighboring classrooms can be stark and demonstrates one of the most important difficulties in delivering the best education: variations in teacher quality.

We all have memories of teachers who created unique environments and communities of learners. Some teachers (hopefully) were positive and stimulating, some forgettable most likely, and others just downright boring or even demeaning. A lot of people have memories of both extremes that stick with them for life. Whether a teacher is a warm, fuzzy person or a strict disciplinarian doesn't matter as much as the teacher's ability to create appropriately challenging, meaningful learning opportunities while providing guidance along the way. Perhaps most important is that teachers believe in their students' capacity for learning and have a drive to reach each individual.

Sadly, not all teachers believe in their students' ability to learn. Or they are just too overwhelmed to put forth the extra effort sometimes needed to help individuals grasp a lesson. This disparity starts with teachers' own experiences as children in school, which often vastly differs from the experiences of their students, especially for teachers working in high-poverty schools. Some people have trouble understanding that just because they were self-motivated and did well in school, not all children experience the same drive and level of success, let alone support. Teacher certification programs can further widen disparities in teacher quality because they don't always emphasize the importance of honestly believing in students' capabilities and backing up that belief with appropriate action—teaching lessons that engage students' minds. In a nutshell, not all teacher preparation programs are created equally.

Teaching the Teacher

Teachers are all college graduates, and a required prerequisite for receiving state certification (except in special circumstances) is completion of a teacher preparation program at an accredited institution. However, teachers' journeys into the profession are not all the same. The differences in teacher preparation programs are complex, and a full description is beyond the scope of this book. But based on my own experience, and what I have learned from other teachers over the years, discrepancies in program length, amount of actual classroom experience, and type of education courses are significant contributors to disparities in teacher quality.

When I was studying to become a teacher, my program started in January and included one quarter of mostly education courses supplemented with a few days a week in a classroom where I assisted and occasionally taught lessons. Spring and fall quarters, I spent half of each day student teaching and the other half taking classes. By the last quarter, I was teaching full-time. The immersive nature of the program gave me the opportunity to gain a wealth of actual teaching experience. I was able to see how school dynamics change over the course of a full year: the excitement of the fall, the stress of report cards and holidays, winter darkness and classroom cultures in full swing (both the positive and not-so-positive aspects), spring testing and more stress, spring fever and the anticipation of summer. All of these dynamics can affect the behavior of both adults and children and, as a result, the flow of daily routines.

Other teacher preparation programs are not as immersive. Prospective teachers can graduate with limited experience in actual classrooms—sometimes as little as six weeks, with a smattering of other days. Like anyone else perfecting a skill, student teachers need practice to become proficient. They also need guidance and constructive feedback on a daily basis from mentor teachers. What level of proficiency can realistically be acquired in six weeks' time? How much can student teachers learn and incorporate from mentors in a matter of a few months? It seems only logical that the more experience student teachers have, the better prepared they'll be for a teaching position. But not all teacher preparation programs abide by this logic—thus contributing to the disparity between classrooms and schools. And, ultimately, it's the students who suffer.

Further deepening the disparity, some schools are hiring teachers who have not completed an accredited teacher certification program at all. Certain "high needs" areas, such as mathematics, science, special education, and English language learning (ELL)—also known as English as a second language (ESL)—lack qualified teachers, so some districts will go to great lengths to fill those vacant positions. Some award emergency teaching certificates to people as long as they have a college degree. These new hires can then earn their teaching certification through weekend and evening courses or online programs while they are teaching students.

Why is this a problem? An expert scientist does not necessarily make an expert science teacher. Highly skilled, successful professionals often cannot remember what it is like to not understand the basics of their field. For example, as an undergrad taking college algebra, my teacher was a graduate student who was supposedly a brilliant mathematician. He spent almost every minute of class writing and solving problems on the board with his back to us. When he was done, he would briefly turn around, ask if there were any questions, assign homework, and then class would be over. His approach to teaching wasn't very effective. Yet if this "brilliant mathematician" wanted to teach high school math today in a district with a vacant position, he would be hired immediately.

Districts are often caught in a bind—either hire teachers where needed, whether certified or not, or have overcrowded classrooms with qualified teachers. Districts will likely continue to face this conundrum until teaching is a more appealing profession to college graduates, one that is actually respected and provides more lucrative compensation. Bottom line, whether teachers are receiving their training while on the job or prior to entering the profession, teacher education programs do not address pedagogy, the method and practice of teaching, with the same depth. Often it is simply assumed that being a good student will translate into being a good teacher. Thus some essential elements of quality teaching are not emphasized. But with students' futures at stake, it's critical for us to know what those essential elements are, and for teachers to be able to incorporate them into classroom routines.

Elements of Effective Instruction

There is an art and science to teaching. Teachers need to know their students, the instructional content, and methods for reaching all students. It is also important to remember the human element of working with children, like how important a genuine smile can be, how everyone has a need to be seen and have their voice heard, or how something as simple as the weather—snow falling outside—can create a level of excitement in the classroom that changes the flow of a lesson. Effective instruction is complex. At a minimum, teachers should have a firm grasp of the following:

- The individual lesson content and objectives

- How to create different experiences to teach the same content; for example, reading a newspaper instead of a story excerpt in a textbook to practice summarizing, or using biographies and other literature to learn about history instead of just a textbook

- Prior knowledge the students need for the lesson to be successful; for example, knowing how to count before learning to add or knowing letters and sounds before reading

- Future application and use of the content; for example, learning how adjectives modify nouns, thus using them to make writing more expressive

- Each student's current abilities, skills, and knowledge, and how to bridge the gap between where they are and the prior knowledge they need to learn a lesson, if necessary (which is more often than not)

- How to keep a group of children focused, disciplined, and behaving respectfully toward themselves and each other

- How to treat the students with respect

- Instructional methods that can account for different learning styles

- An understanding of child development and how that affects instruction

- How to objectively assess whether a student "gets it"

- How to create an atmosphere that fosters inquiry and a joy of learning

- The ability to challenge students at all skill levels

When you consider all the knowledge and skills teachers must have in order to create a successful learning environment, it becomes obvious why disparities in teacher training programs—and the hiring of teachers who have not completed one at all—are of great concern.

We Don't All Learn the Same

The last point in the preceding list about challenging students at all skill levels can be particularly difficult to master because it requires teachers to understand the level of complex thought required to complete a task. Bloom's taxonomy articulates different levels of cognitive demand in order of difficulty: remembering, understanding, applying, analyzing, evaluating, and creating.

For example, let's say students read a book about the Roaring Twenties in the United States. Remembering refers to the students' ability to recall specific information directly from the text, perhaps that the story is set in the US in 1920. To achieve the next level, understanding, students must figure out what the author is trying to say. For example, they might surmise that the author wants the reader to understand the connection between World War I and the Roaring Twenties. To apply the material, they must use their understanding of the text in another way; for example, relating the unregulated postwar boom of the twenties to the Depression of the 1930s. Analyzing requires the students to deepen their understanding, perhaps comparing and contrasting the book to other texts on a related topic. Evaluating is a high-level cognitive task that examines information to discern the author's purpose; for example, does the author's belief in government regulations affect their portrayal of the glut of the 1920s? Creating requires students to question how their thinking has changed after reading the text; for example, asking themselves how they look differently at the years after World War I than they did before reading the text.

Being aware of those levels of thinking and complexities can help teachers plan experiences that incorporate an appropriate mix of cognition in order to effectively teach to the diversity of learners in classrooms. Though it is important to make sure students have a good foundation—for example, establishing that they understand what the text is saying before asking them to compare and contrast to a different text—too much of instruction, especially in low-performing schools, dwells in the remembering and understanding levels, and students don't get opportunities to delve deeper. (Thus a lot of boredom.)

Conversely, it is just as detrimental to learning if the lesson is too advanced. It makes sense that you wouldn't teach advanced calculus to students who are just learning about fractions. Quality teaching takes a student from where they are and helps them learn and grow from that point. Learning theory, specifically Vygotsky's zone of proximal development, articulates that students have certain limits to where they can be stretched, and teachers should be aware of those limits.[6]

Howard Gardner's work defining multiple intelligences—the different ways people learn, process, and share knowledge—is also helpful for planning learning experiences that incorporate different modalities. Simply put, lecture-style instruction, which is very common, doesn't reach all students. Providing a variety of kinesthetic (movement and touch), visual (images and spatial understanding), and auditory (music and sound) experiences can help more students learn the content.

One middle school social studies teacher I knew did a weeklong unit on multiple intelligences. Students did presentations about their learning strengths; some acted out scenes, some created songs, some wrote essays, and some painted. Not only did the students uncover their strengths, but they also had the opportunity to discover other people's learning styles, which helped build community among them. The students were also encouraged to utilize skills that were not their particular strengths. For example, an articulate student who had superior auditory skills painted a picture instead of giving an oral presentation. Throughout the year, students incorporated the information about multiple intelligences into what they were learning.

Learning from the Brain

One area I learned a little bit about during my career was brain research. Without trying to explain the topic in depth, which I'm not qualified to do anyway, there are two main concepts that stick with me. The first is that children learn better when starting with concrete experiences, and then moving into the abstract. An example is how six-year-olds in first grade learn about elephants and other non-domesticated animals. Typically, students will read stories, look at pictures, and maybe even watch a film about elephants. They might even be assigned a report. Then, after all the abstract learning (imagining what a two-ton animal is like from an 8½ x 11-inch photo is quite abstract), the class goes to the zoo and the children see how large an elephant actually is, how they move around, smell, and sound. Brain research says take the field trip first to build a schema, or foundation, and then abstract connections can be made. Suddenly they have a much better frame of reference for learning about elephants and the classroom activities make a lot more sense.

The second point that sticks with me is that learning is better retained over time when skills are repeatedly used in different situations. This means that more Ditto sheets practicing multiplication problems don't really work. Students need to use multiplication in different contexts so they can understand when to multiply and how to get the correct answer. The idea being that new connections in the brain won't be accessible over time without repetition of applying the skills in a variety of settings, as well as reflecting on the learning—use it or lose it.

Effective teaching requires knowledge, conscious effort, and lots of practice. Successfully integrating elements of effective instruction into teaching practice does not just *happen*. It requires positive support during internships (student teaching), knowledgeable principals, and ongoing professional development. University programs vary in how they prepare teachers. Thus, some new teachers are adept at the art and science of teaching while some experienced teachers struggle every day, and vice versa, depending on their experiences and the level of ongoing support they receive. Teachers' success can also depend on how well barriers to student learning are addressed—or even acknowledged.

Barriers to Effective Instruction

Perhaps one of the biggest barriers to quality instruction that teachers inflict on themselves is to make assumptions about how their students learn based on their own experiences. Unfortunately, many teachers assume students can and should learn the same way they did when they were in school—mostly through lecture (an auditory style of teaching)—and that something is wrong with students if they don't understand a concept after being told. When teachers make assumptions like this, they don't take the time to reflect on how their own instructional style could be part of the problem, and they don't take into account different learning styles, or the many other possible reasons students aren't getting the material—even just boredom.

One statement I used to hear often in teaching workshops usually went something like this: "My students won't understand that. They can learn only when I teach it a certain way." But assuming that children can only learn in one particular way is limiting . . . and just plain wrong. To feel that students won't learn unless a teacher directly tells them something doesn't take into account that students also learn by *doing*. The statement "I assume they don't know and that they won't learn unless I tell them" undermines students' abilities to make sense of an experience—a skill they've been using since they were infants. And it certainly doesn't acknowledge that children learn from each other. "Psst, if you just do this, then you get the answer." Children tend to achieve at the level adults believe they can reach. They will often rise to the level adults expect, or not try if expectations are low. It is up to adults to keep classrooms both positive and appropriately challenging for all learners. Making faulty assumptions about students' capabilities is a disservice to them and benefits neither students nor teachers.

Another obstacle that prevents effective instruction is pressure from administration to emulate a teaching method simply because it works in another school or classroom. (This "success story" line of reasoning is often used to adopt new programs, too.) Some people argue that emulating successful methods will work for everyone everywhere. But that seems to discount the human element of education. We are not all alike. We develop differently, and we all have various influences from birth. Teachers are not carbon copies of each other, even if they use the same resources for instruction. (Remember the two different math teachers depicted at the opening of this chapter?) While similarities do exist, every cohort of students is unique and has different needs. Siblings, even twins, have unique attributes and often do not have the same learning styles or interests. The belief that an eight-year-old child in one school will learn the same material with exactly the same instruction as an eight-year-old child in another school is just not realistic.

This unrealistic expectation is compounded by another one—the desire for instant results. Frustration and skepticism inevitably ensue when the new text series or teaching method does not deliver on its lofty promises. (Remember the complexities of phasing in a new text in chapter 2? The new language and structure take time for both teachers and students to adjust to.) Inevitably, results don't meet the expectations. Support tends to wane after a couple of years. Teachers tend to revert to whatever method and material they are comfortable teaching. A new administrator comes along within a few years and says something like, "If we just did XYZ, like they did in Other School District, our test scores would rocket sky-high!"

Cue the groans and eye rolls.

After experiencing this vicious cycle a few times, many teachers close their doors on learning anything new. They know that administration will change again in a few years, bringing with it changes in policy and program, so why bother? While I understand the inclination, refusing to try out new methods leads to stagnation and apathy, which trickle down to the students.

It is often helpful to observe and explore different ways of teaching, yet such an endeavor must be approached with genuine curiosity, and teachers must integrate new methods into their own particular style, rather than blindly adopt someone else's. Trying out new approaches, like different questioning strategies or using hands-on materials in mathematics, is important to teachers' continuing education—just like our students, we always need to be learning! Plus, many people need to see something modeled before they can visualize it. (Teachers have different learning styles just like children.) But mimicking a strategy, no matter how much it's touted, is often not sustainable or effective.

I'll leave you with one final thought about emulating "success." A big downside to this is that often all we see is the "success" part, not the sacrifices, mistakes, and misjudgments that were made along the way. For example, Jaime Escalante was a highly successful mathematics teacher in a tough part of Los Angeles. He was remarkably gifted in many ways, especially in helping students prepare for and pass advanced placement exams. He inspired countless students and other educators. (There is even a movie about him: *Stand and Deliver.*) Yet he also had more than one heart attack and was away from his family many, many nights.

We as a society often sacrifice sleep and family time for the sake of work. I did this also and wish I had found a better balance. A lot of people admired for their achievements also have family they ignore, friends they never see, or health they neglect so they can focus on work—on accomplishments. While teaching children to strive for success is important, what is just as important, if not more so, is modeling balance in life—among work, family, healthy activities, daily chores, and unexpected occurrences.

We all—parents, educators, and administrators—have a responsibility to make public schools vibrant places of learning. To do that, we must take the time to reflect on the barriers we unnecessarily inflict on students— obsession with success, false assumptions about how and what children are capable of learning, or lack of awareness about the basics of good teaching. When we can acknowledge these barriers and explore ways to overcome them, positive learning communities can flourish; in other words, schools can be a place where children feel valued and respected.

Positive Learning Communities

It's up to individual teachers to create a positive learning community in the classroom—an environment that fosters growth both academically and socially. This isn't something most people talk about when they discuss school reform. It's easier to focus on textbooks and test scores— tools we can uniformly implement and assess—but in the absence of an environment that feels nurturing and safe, children generally do not flourish. If we're serious about ensuring all students receive a quality education, then we must consider the type of environment in which children learn and how teachers shape that environment.

There's no one way to creative a positive learning community, but in my experience, the key is to acknowledge two basic human needs— to feel safe and to belong. So much of children's lives is out of their control, and many have lives that are chaotic outside of school. When children feel safe, when they feel like they are valued members of a community, they are more likely to express themselves, feel motivated to do their best, and actually take the risk of learning something new. Children sense sincerity and will more often than not strive to do well for a teacher who is honest, believes in their abilities, holds them to standards, seeks to connect with them in a meaningful way, and fosters an environment that is both safe and inclusive.

Belonging in the Classroom

From day one of each school year, I did my best to create a feeling of belonging. I started by putting up student work around the classroom. Some educators emphasize the importance of instructional bulletin boards and that everything should have a clear educational purpose. You see all sorts of lists about rules, informational charts, and decorative or "inspirational" posters (remember that orange cat—"Hang in there, baby"?). These can sometimes be helpful. But something I learned over the years—although I did create all sorts of displays as well—was that the more I let students decorate and take responsibility for our shared space, the more the classroom became a community, and thus much more conducive to learning.

Gangs

It is the sense of belonging that is part of the appeal of gangs. They offer a sense of family and identity to those children who have turbulent, unsafe, or neglectful home lives. More information can be found at violencepreventioninstitute. com or gangfree.org.

One thing I liked to do was tell students that they could put anything they wanted up on the bulletin board (or whatever space we had for artwork)—with the parameters of no sex, drugs, or violence. That was usually met with a few groans and mischievous grins, but I had only to remind them that we were in school and to ask, "Would you like to share that with the principal?" Point made.

Not only did this activity save me time, but also the room became *our* space—not just mine. As the first few weeks went on, I would continue to post student work and other things I felt were important, but gradually I would also begin to post photos of the students. The photos were candid shots of the students working. The intention behind this was for students to see themselves as learners, not posers or clowns. Supporting this aspect of their self-image was important, especially for those students who didn't think of themselves as being bright, or whose brightness was actively discouraged at home, where they were labeled as "nerds" or "geeks" or "know-it-alls" or accused of acting "white" (more common than you might think). Plus, putting up photos just added to the welcoming student-centered atmosphere.

While teaching eighth-grade mathematics, part of the first lesson in each class was to measure the bulletin board and figure out how to divide the area into five equal parts, one for each class. They then had to divide their class space into equal areas for each student in the class, usually between twenty-eight and thirty-two students. Next, they decided what dimensions would be reasonable for a piece of artwork. They were then given the rest of that first class to create something to display.

Though some students complained initially that it was weird (and they were right—it was definitely unusual to draw in math class!), this bulletin board quickly became a center of attraction. Students who were talented artists (there were always a few) got the opportunity to show off their skill to their peers, who were usually curious to see what their friends, classmates, and crushes had made. Students hung out in the room in between classes to look at the art, and later at the candid photos—pretty remarkable for an eighth grader to choose to be in a classroom and not in the hall where all the action is!

Most of us, at some point in our lives, can recall feeling out of place in a group. Perhaps you were laughed at for something you said. Maybe everyone just ignored your input or you had the sinking sense no one appreciated your contributions. Contrast those unpleasant memories with being in a place where others welcomed you, where people listened to you, and laughed *with* you. In which situation did you learn more, were you happier? It doesn't take a lot of effort to create an inclusive atmosphere for students, to give them the opportunity to be authentic with each other and express themselves creatively. While a positive environment that embraces students' individuality is preferable to one that demands conformity, it doesn't prevent misbehavior. How the teacher deals with classroom misbehavior is an important part of the learning environment.

Classroom Management (a.k.a. Discipline)

A big part of what goes on in schools is about keeping chaos from taking over. In most schools, student demographics have changed over the years. The population is more ethnically and economically diverse than it was twenty-five years ago. However, one thing that hasn't changed is the importance of maintaining a safe learning environment.

I strongly believe that a positive community atmosphere with engaging lessons will keep students focused on learning and away from running amok more often than not. Some people may disagree, and many classrooms work well with other teaching and discipline styles. However, if students are to explore different ways to make sense of the world and their place in it, a safe and supportive atmosphere is more conducive to creativity than one where students are fearful and their voices are squashed.

How a teacher engages students and keeps "order" is a part of teaching that is often not spoken about. If classrooms are not functioning well, if constant power struggles and frequent distractions are common, then less learning of content happens. Some schools have school-wide discipline policies for each class to follow, while others leave it up to individual teachers to manage. Yet even with building policies in place, teachers often implement them differently.

Class rules can tell you something about teachers.

Rules set up the community, and rules that emphasize the negative are not the most conducive to learning, plus they're usually obvious— for example, not talking or getting out of your seat without permission, not chewing gum, and not running. My classroom rules focused less on individual behaviors and more on global guidelines for a variety of contexts. I "borrowed" these rules from an associate professor. They were based on three values: commitment, courtesy, and cooperation. I liked them because they were simple, positive, and appropriate for pretty much any situation, negating the need for a lengthy list of dos and don'ts. I strived to create an atmosphere focused on learning rather than punitive measures. As one friend would ask students, "Do you want me to deal with your intelligence or your behavior?"

However, many teachers use a more heavy-handed approach to keep students in line. For example, one middle school math teacher I worked with would allow only two bathroom passes per student for each quarter (about ten weeks). If they didn't use them, they would get extra credit. He would write up students and send them to the office if they didn't bring a pencil after a third warning. (No pens for math.) Sadly, he would also yell loudly at students and sometimes even get in their faces. His strict policies meant he didn't have problems with students hanging out in the bathroom and that most everyone brought pencils, but he also created a fearful environment that was counterproductive to learning for many students.

Contrast that approach with mine. I was in the room next door also teaching mathematics. In my classroom, bathroom visits were definitely allowed and only a rare few times did students abuse the privilege. I also insisted on pencils for math, but I would "sell" the students a pencil for a nickel, and more often than not, I would "sell" it to them on credit. (A couple of students would give me a quarter and say, "That is for the next few times, Mr. G.") I wanted them to spend more time thinking about math rather than fretting about writing implements.

And, perhaps, my approach was self-serving in a way—it was easier for me to focus on teaching mathematics when I didn't have to obsess over whether students were following a bunch of arbitrary rules. And I believe a majority of my students learned a lot as a result. If you feel safe, you are more likely to ask good questions and focus your mind on learning.

Of course, some days teaching felt more like trying to nail warm Jell-O to the wall—nothing was sticking. Sometimes things did not go smoothly, no matter how positive my approach to managing the classroom. Sometimes I reprimanded students. Sometimes I lost my cool. It goes with the territory of being a teacher, no matter how skilled and even-tempered you are. But if you let them, those fraught moments can teach you something about yourself, the students, and classroom discipline.

For example, once one of my sixth-grade students was struggling to get started on an assignment. She was rummaging noisily through the clutter in her desk for pencil and paper. I told her to get going on the assignment a couple of times, yet still she poked around in her desk, creating a racket.

Very tersely I said, "Get your act together. You're wasting time!"

"I can't find a pencil! Leave me alone!" she said.

Well, I wasn't going to take that. "You need to get it together *now* and start your work!" I spewed.

She suddenly got up and ran to the door, shouting, "I'm leaving! I hate you!" and slamming it behind her. The rest of the class was still as could be. My heart pounded. I felt like a complete fool. I had blown it.

After a few moments, I apologized to the rest of the class. Luckily, the students were forgiving. Unfortunately, I never got a chance to apologize to the girl, because she and her mother moved that very day, which, as it turned out, was likely why she was so upset. I'm still haunted by the fact that I added to her trauma. That day, my student desperately needed the experience of a positive learning community and I failed to provide it. It was a reminder to me that students have lives outside of school that have a huge effect on their behavior in the classroom, something that's easy to forget when a student is not cooperating. But rather than reacting in anger, more often than not, it's compassion that's called for—a lesson that I learned the hard way.

One other charged experience that stuck with me over the years happened while I was teaching eighth-grade math. A student challenged me about the solution to a problem. I knew I was right. She knew she was right. I got a little louder. She got a little louder. We got so loud that a teacher across the hall came over, gave me the stink eye, and closed my door. The next day I apologized to the class. My students were gracious. "No problem, Mr. G. We got your back," one of them said. As for the girl I argued with, she transferred out of the school.

Why did I feel the need to get into a power struggle with her? To defend my right answer, my ego? My behavior that day contradicted my belief that students should be able to ask questions and form their own opinions. Who knows what was going on in that girls' home life, why she felt the need to oppose me? As a teacher, it does not pay to be reactionary, and it behooves everyone when you check your ego at the door—after all, students are there to *learn*, not to make us teachers feel good about ourselves. I've found that when teachers make classroom management missteps, a sincere apology goes a long way. While it's preferable to avoid these gaffes altogether, they provide an opportunity to role model how to behave when you *do* blunder, which we all do. Apologizing also reminds students that you value their perspective—an important part of creating a positive learning community.

Believing Students Can Succeed

In addition to creating a sense of belonging in the classroom and maintaining order in a positive way, believing that *all* children can learn is key to their success. Did you have a teacher who believed in you? How did that affect your achievement? Many successful adults have stories of teachers who believed in their abilities and how that made a positive difference in their lives. (Many of us had teachers who were quite the opposite, unfortunately.)

Though one teacher may be seemingly strict and another more relaxed, it is the belief that each individual can learn and the effort to teach them that is more important to student success. Holding students accountable and requiring completed work on time are two important ways that teachers show they believe in their students.

Consider the following three examples. While teaching styles vary, the instructors who believed in their students' ability to learn are the ones who created a successful learning environment.

Mr. Hamilton, a high school physics teacher with fifteen years' experience, was helping students prepare for project presentations. He taught at a high school in an area that was transitioning from a mostly middle- to low-income rural population to a more diverse population with numerous new housing developments and inexpensive rentals.

"Mr. Hamilton, how do we show the results of our experiment?" inquired a student in one of the groups.

"What do you think would make it clear? What are you *really* trying to show?" replied Mr. Hamilton.

"Oh, I hate it when you answer a question with another question!" one of the other group members blurted out. Mr. Hamilton just smiled and walked away.

When I asked another student if Mr. Hamilton did that often, she said, "All the time! He is always encouraging us to ask better questions, so he answers most questions with other questions. I'm learning, but it drives me crazy!" I also asked her if the class got out of hand ever. She replied that they are so busy with classwork, no one has time to goof off; though she did say that at the beginning of the year, a few students got kicked out for disruptions.

Like Mr. Hamilton, Ms. Fredericks had fifteen years' experience, though mostly with second and third graders. When I knew her, she happened to be teaching sixth grade in a tough school. (When you have a group of twenty-nine eleven- to thirteen-year-olds in one room, it's challenging to keep chaos at bay.) Academically, her students had a wide range of abilities; for example, they were reading anywhere from a second-grade to a ninth-grade level. She was known for loving her students but also for being tough with discipline. She held them accountable for their work, and she had no tolerance for fooling around. Typically, she kept about a half-dozen or so students in for recess each day because of misbehavior. Yet one of her students once said, "Some people think she's mean, but she doesn't let things get out of control. She really cares if we learn."

Ms. Brown had even more years of experience than Mr. Hamilton and Ms. Fredericks—over twenty. She taught fifth grade in a school where 75 percent of the students received free lunch or paid reduced prices, a school where about forty languages other than English were spoken in homes. In addition to her years of experience, Ms. Brown also had an administration credential. She wanted to be a principal. Though she tried to keep control of her class, her students just ignored her. She tried to teach quality lessons, but often dumbed down the content. "These kids just don't have the skills to learn," she once said. She spent an inordinate amount of time on discipline and didn't seem to believe in their ability to learn; though she obviously cared and tried.

Three different teachers and styles, yet only two of them were successful. The common thread between the more successful teachers is their belief in students' ability to learn and their commitment to making learning accessible to all students, no matter the resources. Students who have teachers who believe in their abilities tend to believe in themselves, and self-confidence is an important part of being successful in any endeavor.

Sometimes It's the Little Things

Everything that happens in a day, no matter how big or small, even thirty-second activities waiting for a bell to ring, can be important to a community of students. Side comments, how teachers react to children's comments to each other, and how routines are managed all can make a day productive and positive—or not.

Sometimes it is the simplest of actions that can aid student learning. For example, I taught sixth grade in a portable building for a few years, which provided opportunities for activities that couldn't happen in the main building. The room was barely big enough for us all. Twenty-seven to thirty-four sixth graders, their desks, and their chairs filled up a 25 x 35-foot area quickly. Add a teacher's desk, an overhead projector, a table with two Apple IIe computers, a couple of bookshelves, and open space became scarce. The airflow was limited—a door on one side and three 2 x 3-foot slat windows on the other were the only places where air could slip in. The door side had three large (4 ft. wide x 6 ft. tall) fixed "windows" made of indestructible yet scratchable plastic; it was like looking through the windshield of a car left sitting under a sappy tree for a couple of years—light came through and you could make out figures on the other side, but you couldn't call it transparent. They were used to display a lot of student work.

Sometimes the energy inside the portable was just too much, so we would take a couple of laps around it. Amazing what three minutes of movement and breathing can do for a person, let alone a small herd of hormonally unbalanced, antsy eleven- to thirteen-year-olds. There were lots of smiles and feelings of enjoying a simple moment as the stream of bodies bounded down the four steps to the ground, snaked around the small building a few times, and then back inside. We would then get back to the business at hand. I'm not sure how that would be received now in a time when administrators are spouting phrases like "Every minute, every day, every way," referring to a focus on academics (mostly math and reading). Yet I guess they would encourage the idea if they could step back from the pressure of test scores to see the level of focus in the room after we took the time to move around a bit.

Ironically, we know the connection between physical health and mental acuity. However, recess and physical education are looked at as extras—like the arts. Direct reading and math instruction is usually considered more important. Yet students, actually all people, think clearer when they engage in daily movement. Oxygen and blood flow are essential for the brain. Breathing and moving increases the ability of anyone to stay calm and focused.

There were some individuals who took laps as a reprimand because they would get so antsy that they not only disrupted others but obviously weren't learning themselves. Thus, a couple of laps would help relieve a little stress. Some students were aware of their need to move: "Mr. Green, I need to take a lap" was heard a few times. I would often agree, although there were times when it was obviously a way to avoid work.

Troublemaker

I spent a lot of effort myself as a student avoiding work and being a smart aleck. That is part of why my teacher's desk was always at the back or side of the class. It not only left the front of the room open for teaching but also made the few times I would sit there interesting. Sometimes it was hard not to laugh at students who thought they were getting away with passing a note or sneaking candy.

Sometimes I would have a child do some push-ups: "Drop and give me ten." This was said with a smile, and some of the children enjoyed doing the push-ups. They also got a kick when I would do the push-ups with them (or even sometimes by myself). The first time I asked a student to do push-ups, I'd do them too to ease any possible tension or embarrassment. (I also chose students carefully, knowing who would react in a positive way to my push-up request and who wouldn't.) Relieving tension with a sense of humor was the goal of my asking them to do push-ups. Of course it was not for every situation, but it was just one of the small things I did that could have a big effect on the classroom dynamic.

I am not saying that running around a portable or doing push-ups should be incorporated into every classroom. Far from it. It worked for me because it was part of my style. There are lots of creative teachers using many other ways to keep their learning communities going, using effective and wonderful methods that fit their style. I believe that the art of teaching comes from within. While methods can be learned from "experts," the hundreds of decisions that teachers make every hour have to be genuine to who they are. Children know when things are contrived or phony. That is when they tune out or rebel.

Other small actions like playing at recess came naturally to me. One, I love to play active games like basketball, four square, and softball. The children seemed to enjoy watching their teacher in a coat (quickly tossed aside) and tie run around and play. (I think it is hard for adults to remember how some children can't imagine teachers as regular people.) In addition to having fun, playing at recess also presented the opportunity for me to witness other aspects of the children, like who would take charge in games, how games were played, or what kids were loners, and who hung out with whom. All the while they were seeing other aspects of me, like how I could laugh while being taken out in four square.

A lot of the boys liked playing with and challenging me in various sports. So many children, especially those living in poverty, don't have many positive male role models, and with elementary schools, in particular, being places where men are often scarce, the novelty of my presence outside was even more apparent and appreciated. The playground supervisors, usually part-time employees whose authority was often challenged, also liked having me outside. Having another adult present and visible helped prevent a lot of playground conflicts. The children also saw that I had fun and genuinely enjoyed being with them, that I wasn't always in a hurry to escape to the staff room. (Though I did enjoy those breaks often as well.)

Back inside the classroom, I found small actions were quite effective in getting students' attention and reminding them that you cared. Early on as a student teacher, I was amazed at how quickly students would focus on what was being written on the board. My mentor teacher would write a couple of directions, for example, *Clear off your desks and get out your reading book*, or a note of praise such as *I like how you all are working quietly on the math.* All praise was tied to an action and was genuine. It was a quick nonverbal method of getting students' attention.

I utilized the power of writing notes on the board or overhead a lot. It saved my voice and worked well. Notes like *After you finish your math, get out your pleasure book and read silently*, or upon returning to class after an assembly: *The way you all handled the assembly was so impressive. Everyone listened respectfully and applauded appropriately. I'm very proud to be your teacher! Love, Mr. Green.* The students would be so curious that any rowdy behavior settled down while they tried to predict what I was writing. I didn't have to speak at all, just point to the board.

I would also write personalized Post-its and sporadically stick them on students' desks. *You help the class a lot with your good questions.* Or simply, *I'm glad you are here today.* Once I was shown the possibility, it came naturally and I believe it made a difference to take just a few moments to write positive messages. The smiles I received supported that belief. We all like to be acknowledged. Everyone likes to receive praise—especially when it is sincere.

All the little actions described above helped me forge a meaningful connection with my students. They also helped create what I hoped was a positive learning atmosphere. Meaningful connections start with being genuine and develop into taking simple actions that show caring. I strived to let students know I cared about their learning but also saw them as people. The projects and activities I did, like the ones described in Chapter 2, would not have been as successful without the little actions I took to help us bond.

Rewards and Entitlement

Many schools and teachers believe in rewarding good behavior, yet sometimes offering extrinsic rewards for being on time, saying please and thank you, and holding a door open fosters a sense of entitlement in young people, where they expect a bonus for just being a polite human.

Connecting with Students: Reflecting, Writing, Sharing

Teachers can use different methods to connect with students and encourage them to develop strong relationships with each other. One of the ways I did this was through journal writing. Children, like everyone, have a need to find their voice, to be heard and acknowledged. Writing is a quiet activity that requires us to reflect upon ourselves without being interrupted by others. In a world with so much noise, quiet reflection can help us clarify our thoughts, uncover feelings, and even explore dreams. A talented teacher and friend of mine helped me to structure the journaling exercises in a way that encouraged the kids to open up.

When I used journaling exercises in my elementary and middle school classes (even math class sometimes), I would ask the students to start with "Dear Journal" to establish the sense of an intimate dialogue. Then I would introduce the writing prompt of the day, for example, "Now I understand . . ." or "I am the river . . ." or "Today I . . ." or some other open-ended question to get students going. I would respond to the prompt as well, writing on the overhead (not switched on yet) to model. We would write for two minutes straight with the only requirement being that pens and pencils always be moving, even if students were only writing, "Blah, blah, blah."

Sharing their writing with the class could be intimidating, so often I would go first to help the class feel more comfortable. Then a few bold students would raise their hands, and when the rest of the class listened respectfully, more and more students participated. It was very moving to have children listen to each other, and the honest communication helped build a family atmosphere in the classroom. After a few weeks we'd have to limit the amount of sharing because so many wanted to be heard. (I tried to make sure that everyone got to share at least once a week if they wanted.) Not everyone was comfortable reading aloud, so sometimes students would ask me or another classmate to read their entry. Those who didn't want theirs read aloud at all (though almost all of those shy students eventually shared their work) knew, however, that I would read them later. I did give them the option not to share everything with me, but no one kept me from reading any entries. It was important for me to read each entry and respond with care. They knew they were being listened to.

As time went on, more and more risks were taken as students opened up; for example, by sharing some intimate thoughts about themselves and their families. We had some emotional, serious, silly, and hilarious moments, which often were descriptions of mishaps involving siblings. The expectation of courtesy was met, and the kids opened up. Every once in a while, snide comments were made (they are children after all). When this happened, I (or sometimes another student) would respond with something like "That is rude, crude, unattractive, and socially unacceptable" (a favorite line I got from my mentor teacher—it just rolls off the tongue). This is an example of how I would discipline with humor, as it was not spoken with anger. The atmosphere was one of trust and honesty, so during those times it only took a little reminder to be able to move on.

Every year I dealt with some smart-alecky wannabe comedians. Some students would do just about anything to be heard, and interrupting was a common issue for many. I would remind them about the importance of timing. "As every good comedian knows— timing, timing, timing—is the key to any good act. And now is not the time for that." Common courtesy and respecting others are important aspects of being in a group/community.

Sharing journal entries was just one way community was established in my classroom. We all want to be heard (part of why social media is so prevalent and powerful), and finding one's voice is an important aspect of life. Being able to stand up for what you believe in (after you figure out what that is) and articulate your truth can build self-esteem. People who feel good about themselves are generally more positive and productive in their communities and classrooms.

An Opportunity to Create

Every year teaching was different, even when teaching the same grade. That was part of what made my career so refreshing and challenging. After over a dozen years teaching in one district and a summer of searching for a new challenge in a different school district, I was hired to teach a fifth- and sixth-grade class at an elementary school starting at the beginning of October. The class was created to handle the overcrowding in the fifth- and sixth-grade classes. The principal, against the wishes and recommendations of the teachers, decided it should be made up of students who had moved to the school within the last year or so, which made for an interesting conglomeration of ten- to twelve-year-olds. One of the things that the students and I had in common immediately was that none of us had a long history with the school or neighborhood.

One day, a friend and fellow educator, Kevin, who had just put on a couple of wonderful science assemblies at the school, expressed interest in doing a project with my class. He and I both liked creating meaningful, engaging opportunities for students to apply skills learned. We bantered about ideas with the students, and since Kevin had some film experience, we decided to depict what it might have been like for Ryan White on his last day at elementary school. In the mid-1980s, Ryan contracted AIDS from a tainted blood transfusion. The fear of AIDS had created such a fervor at the time that he was kicked out of school.

When Kevin shared the story about how Ryan was infected through no fault of his own, blamed, attacked, and ostracized, the students were touched and excited about creating a film. We started brainstorming story ideas and possible scenes every morning during our journal time. We did this for a few weeks, realizing that a couple of the students had a gift for this and that they should do the writing. So they worked on the script for what we originally thought would be about a six-minute film.

The script called for only a couple of speaking parts, but everyone (except the cameraperson) did get on film. To make sure everyone was actively involved in some role and to make the experience as real as possible, we found job descriptions of filmmaking on the internet. The jobs were scribbled down on pieces of paper placed in a hat, and each student drew one. They could switch jobs as long as there was no fighting. We emphasized finding a job that fit each student's abilities. Certain students fit roles perfectly. From the director, whom everyone respected and liked, to the cast of Ryan and his best friend, to makeup artist, everyone made a contribution doing what suited them best.

The rehearsals and filming were a wonderfully chaotic time, with the director requesting multiple takes to get a shot just right, the makeup artist putting last touches on the actors, the cameraperson suggesting different angles, and the writers making last-minute changes to the script. I'm sure we disrupted neighboring classrooms a bit, but the teachers were mostly tolerant and supportive. About once or twice a week, we worked on rehearsing and filming. About two months later we had a touching twelve-minute film.

Ryan is shown sitting in a corner of the classroom, with little sneers from a couple of the other students, while the rest of the class is working quietly. The teacher is seen reading the newspaper at his desk. The camera pans the classroom, catching glares, students working, and one girl in particular looking sympathetically at Ryan. The phone rings and afterward the teacher grumpily picks up a box and drops it on the floor near Ryan. "Pack up your stuff. Your mom's coming to get you." Ryan then slowly takes things out of his desk, a not-so-tidy mixture of books and papers and then he finds a crumpled Valentine—from the girl across the room. After he packs his box, he quietly leaves without goodbyes.

A great scene happened by chance during the filming. After Ryan walked out the door of the school for the last time, the camera captured the janitor walking behind him with a big rolling garbage can, like he was clearing out the refuse—Ryan. It happened by accident and the director and cameraperson, being creative, kept it in.

Next, the girl who had sent Ryan a Valentine joins him outside, where he is waiting for his mother.

"They say you're going to die. Are you scared, Ryan?" she says.

"Yeah." Long pause.

"Do you think there is a heaven?" she asks.

Another long pause. "Yeah, my mom says there is a heaven. And that's where we all end up."

"I'm going to miss you."

Ryan's mom then pulls up. He slowly puts the box in the backseat and gets in the front. As they drive off, the girl says, "Ryan, will you save me a place in heaven?"

At this point tears were flowing freely for most everyone who saw the film. The experience gave us a shared purpose. Each with their respective jobs, the students learned to work together and support each other. They honed their empathy skills by imagining what Ryan White's last day of school was like, and they got to try activities without embarrassment, like acting or filming. Parents and other community members attended our premiere. The pride that beamed from the children's faces was an absolute joy to behold. They knew they had created something special. The audience gave a rousing ovation, and I heard only positive feedback from those who saw the film. Without the presence of a positive learning community that we established together (through our commitment to cooperate courteously), which became stronger during the process, a project like this film would not have been as successful.

If there is trust and an authentic bond between students and teachers (goes hand in hand with having high expectations, believing in students' ability to learn, speaking the truth, asking appropriate questions, and having a sense of humor—or just being real and human), students tend to perform better. This is the human element that needs to be acknowledged by policy makers, addressed in teacher preparation programs, and supported by administrators if any meaningful improvement is going to happen.

Schools are not factories producing widgets. Schools are where children go to learn about the world, hopefully make some sense of it, and find where they fit in. Genuinely connecting with students through a smile or a kind word, offering encouragement, and holding them accountable for their efforts can be motivating. Human connection could be just what it takes for that future scientist to create a new form of clean energy or for the next Maya Angelou to find her voice.

Chapter 4

Assessment: How Is Learning Measured?

Test Academies

We were all gathered in the library for a meeting no one wanted to attend. In addition to myself, the group included the third-, fourth-, and fifth-grade teachers; the special education teacher; the English language learners (ELL) teacher; the librarian; the principal; and the building math specialist and reading coordinator (staff who work with students and teachers and offer development activities). The principal, Ms. Jenkins, had scheduled the meeting to plan for the test academies that would take place twice a week for the next three months. About as fun as they sound, the test academies were intended to help students prepare for the Washington Assessment of Student Learning (WASL), the all-important standardized test given in April.

At the time, I was an instructional coach who visited multiple elementary schools within the same district to help teachers who were struggling with mathematics instruction. I worked with teachers at this particular school twice a week. Plagued with low test scores from year to year, this school had a high rate of children living in poverty.

About 75 percent of the students received discounted or free meals every day, and over a third of the students' families spoke languages other than English at home. In some ways, low test scores were the least of these students' problems.

Along with the principal and the building reading and math specialists, I had helped to plan this meeting, but I had mixed feelings about it and the whole test academies approach. I had spent many hours working on test items (more on that later in the chapter) with state assessment coordinators, but I didn't like having so much importance put on the test; much of what I tried to do as an instructional coach was help teachers align their *instruction* with standards that were then measured by the tests. When teachers are able to do this consistently, the test isn't such a big deal—it's not something we need an "academy" to prepare for.

"The kids need practice with what the WASL asks them to do," said Ms. Jenkins. She was a serious woman in her midthirties with about three years of experience as a principal. "We need to break all the third to fifth graders up into small groups—each of us will have one. Classroom teachers will only work with their students, and the rest of us will be working with each grade level. That way, groups can be as little as six to nine students."

A couple of classroom teachers smiled and said they liked the notion of teaching a smaller group. Ms. Jenkins went on to explain that we would use the practice-test items released by the state. She doled out notebooks with all the test items and the answers tabbed according to the weeks they would be used.

Ms. Nathaniel, a veteran fifth-grade teacher who had been at that school for five years asked, "Am I still responsible for how *all* my students do on the test, even though I only have seven of them for the test prep?"

"We are all responsible for *all* the students in the school," Ms. Jenkins said sternly before moving on. I was thinking they both had a point, but their exchange also showed how test fever is so draining—and detracts from teaching and learning. Ms. Jenkins then instructed each of us to do the math items ourselves. The building math specialist would help us score the work. As we began to solve the practice items, I overheard several interesting comments.

"I don't remember how to do this. I always hated math," grumbled Ms. Franklin. She had taught third grade at this school for the last six years, after several years in another district.

"They want us to write our answers in words, numbers, *and* pictures? Showing how we solved the problem?" exclaimed the other third-grade teacher, Ms. Rodriguez, who had been at the school for a decade.

I reassured her, and the others, that they could use words *or* numbers *or* pictures to explain their process. Ms. Rodriguez just shook her head, mumbling about it being different. I almost said, but refrained, "Where have you been? This approach has been common for many years now."

Ms. Williams, a fourth-grade teacher with ten years of experience, frowned. "My students won't know how to do this. The new text hasn't covered this yet."

"Man, this is easy. I love how the problems actually apply the skills and aren't just calculating," added a smiling Ms. Pack, a fourth-grade teacher who was in her second year of teaching. "Similar to our new texts."

Contrast that to Ms. Thorpe, a fifth-grade teacher with twelve years of experience. "*That* is exactly what bothers me! I can't stand word problems," she said. Then someone made a side comment about a *Far Side* cartoon where hell's library was full of math word-problem books. That got people chuckling.

The discussion got fairly lively when it came time to check answers and figure out how to score student work. An important goal was to teach the students how to evaluate their own work, so a good understanding of the scoring rubric was necessary. At 7:00 p.m., after three hours of work, everyone went home with varying degrees of understanding about the practice items and many opinions about the process. I left feeling like the teachers had a much better idea of what students go through at test time.

I also felt a little sad—not only about some of the teachers' attitudes toward mathematics but also about their apparent stress of being judged according to their students' scores. The stress induced by fearing low test scores doesn't help anyone. In my role as an instructional specialist, I knew I had to support efforts like test academies, but I was motivated to continue focusing my energy on student learning and quality instruction, trusting that test scores would show positive results.

Understanding Assessment: The Basics of Testing

Types of Assessment

I by no means am qualified to give a comprehensive explanation about assessment or how to measure student knowledge and abilities. Yet I will point out some basic aspects that are important for understanding testing, like the difference between formative and summative assessments. Formative assessments are used to make instructional decisions. They can be as informal as asking students to give a thumbs-up or a thumbs-down about whether they understand a concept. Formative assessments can also be more formal, like a written or oral quiz. Teachers give formative assessments all the time to gather information about how students are receiving lessons. These assessments help teachers plan next steps for instruction; for example, whether to move on after a lesson is complete or provide remediation—or other enrichment opportunities.

Summative assessments are usually given at the end of a unit of study or grading period. They are intended to assess, in general, how much a student has learned during that particular unit or grading period. Midterms and finals are examples of summative tests. When summative assessments are combined with formative data, teachers, students, and parents can tell how a student is doing. However, achievement tests—predominately a form of summative assessment that evaluates what a student knows and is able to do—are how student learning is mostly judged, and these tests are given once a year to all students.

What's in a Quality Achievement Test Item?

Summative, standards-based tests like the WASL or Common Core assessments are not easy to develop. There are three main interconnected considerations when writing a test question. The first is the **content** of the item. What standard is the item trying to measure? Perhaps the standard is a student's ability to identify a fraction in its lowest terms.

The next consideration is the **context** of the item. How is the problem presented? For example, does the item list groups of fractions in a multiple-choice format or does the problem require reading a paragraph that contains several blanks where the lowest-terms fractions need to be placed? Both require the student to *identify* lowest-terms fractions, yet only one requires more reading skills.

The third consideration is the test item's level of **cognitive demand**. (Remember Bloom's taxonomy mentioned in Chapter 3?). For example, the verb *identify* just requires a student to remember (the first level of cognition) what a lowest-term fraction is. Identifying a lowest-term fraction does not require the same thinking skills as a problem that requires students to read a situation and convert several fractions into lowest terms.

The content, context, and cognitive demand of each test item need to align to give a valid measure of a standard. How does this happen? There are several steps involved in creating a test item that will be used, and different committees will often work on the various steps. Some of the major steps are as follows:

- Specifications for content, context, and cognitive demand are developed according to the learning standards

- Test questions are written by one committee

- Another committee reviews for bias and fairness

- Another group reviews the content

- Test items are piloted (given a test run) with a group of students and then scored. Changes to the test items may be made depending on the results.

- Test items are piloted again, followed by more rounds of review

The items themselves are not the problem with assessment, as long as they go through this rigorous process and qualified professionals facilitate test development and assure validity. Many people, including educators, are often surprised to learn how much time (many months) and effort go into creating each test question. All that time and effort is not cheap, either.

The Business of Testing

Mass testing of public-school students is big business. The companies that develop and score the tests are competitive because the business is lucrative. According to a *Washington Post* article from 2015, student testing is a $2 billion business, and these companies spend millions more on lobbying each year.[7] Even the nonprofit Educational Testing Service pays its board of directors for-profit-level salaries. The article reported that the president of the board at the time, Kurt Landgraf, made $1.3 million in 2013. A fact that is a bit grating to me since that's more than my teacher's salary over my career and school budgets are constantly being cut.

Whether nonprofit or not, these companies bid at the state level to supply and score the annual spring test, which causes much hoopla. In most states, the spring test is a mix of multiple-choice items and items that require writing or some other demonstration of work. The multiple-choice items are easily scored by computers, but the written responses, even if typed into a computer, require a person to interpret and score them.

The number of people needed to score tests is large, and an inordinate amount of money is spent to hire teachers to do this. Teachers from across the state work at least a week at a time to score the tests. Their transportation, meals, and lodging are paid for, if necessary, along with their classroom substitutes. Scoring centers are often located in a different state, not necessarily within driving distance, so people are flown in from all over, stay in decent hotels, and get catered lunches. I flew to Michigan and Minnesota, and drove to Olympia (about sixty miles from Seattle) to score tests. I also commuted to a local Seattle hotel (where I got fed well).

When I asked a person from the Office of Superintendent of Public Instruction about the cost of flying me to another state to do this work, he said, "The testing company pays for it all. Don't worry about it." But those costs are built into the contract—public money pays for it. Remember these companies are in business to make money; they aren't developing these tests out of the goodness of their hearts. While it is fun to be treated like a muckety-muck (some would say considering the amount of education teachers have and how valuable our work is, of course we should be treated well and be able to travel in comfort for work), I see the whole process as a big waste of precious dollars. More local work on all aspects of the big test, not in expensive hotels, would be a great start to saving time and money. It would give more local educators an opportunity to be involved because they wouldn't have to leave town.

Since the results of mathematics and reading tests that public school students take once a year are how many judge the effectiveness of schools, it would help if all educators—and the general public—better understood the testing process. Recognizing the amount of care that goes into creating each test question could help ease some negativity about testing in schools and perhaps collectively help us develop a more realistic perspective about evaluating student achievement— understanding that there is more to the picture than just test scores.

High-Stakes Testing

Students in public schools all over the US take some sort of summative, standardized test every year, usually starting in third grade. Most of these tests measure reading and mathematics skills. Each state has its own test and its own standards that the test is intended to measure, though Common Core State Standards in mathematics and reading have been adopted by over forty states, a few territories, and the District of Columbia. Federal law requires states to be accountable for student learning as measured by test scores. Those states that follow Common Core standards use a testing protocol known as Smarter Balanced assessments, which offers optional interim tests to check student progress prior to the "big test."[8]

Despite the widespread adoption of Common Core standards, the politics surrounding how much uniformity there should be in learning standards and exactly what role government should play in education is ever changing. While the details about testing may change, the annual spring assessment is not likely to disappear. My direct experience with testing is only in Washington State; however, many of the issues I bring up are common all over the country.

Every year, third- to eighth-grade students in Washington State are required to take lengthy assessments measuring knowledge and skills. Testing in Washington State, as in other states, follows a particular protocol: In grades three through eight, students are tested in reading and mathematics (based on Common Core standards). In grades four and seven, they are tested in writing, and in grades five and eight they are tested in science. High school students take two end-of-year assessments that mostly evaluate algebra and geometry skills. High schoolers also take tests in reading, writing, and science.

The results of these tests are interpreted and used in different ways depending on the state. In Washington State, high school diplomas are tied to performance on those assessments, which has become a national trend. The media report the results and rank districts and schools. Since the second Bush presidency implemented the Elementary and Secondary Education Act in 2002 (a.k.a. No Child Left Behind), which ties federal funding to the results, test scores have many far-reaching implications.

That law set the goal of all students meeting standards in reading and mathematics by 2014. Yes, that "deadline" has passed, and the goal has yet to be met. One of the controversial aspects of this law was the way it examined the performance of specific subgroups within a school; categories were based on aspects such as race, grade level, gender, students who received free or reduced lunch, and students who were in special education. Each subgroup had to make adequate yearly progress (AYP) toward meeting standards. AYP was based on how many students within a particular subgroup were meeting standards when the law took effect; students in that subgroup then had to demonstrate steady growth in achievement so that by 2014, 100 percent of students were meeting standards. If a school or district did not make AYP, there were progressive warnings and penalties each year, from being put in an "at-risk" category to having federal funds cut.

However, one benefit to this law was that educators had to look at the subgroups that struggle academically. As one university professor put it, "Now they have to pay attention to brown and Black people. You can't just ignore them."

As in any government policy, there are details that are too lengthy to describe here. The main point is that the legislation increased the importance of the annual spring test by linking funding to results. Threatened with penalties if goals were not met, everyone in struggling schools—from administrators to teachers to children—felt even more pressure. A high-stakes, anxiety-ridden environment is not exactly conducive to learning. Is it any surprise then that 100 percent of children are still not meeting standards?

In 2015, the law was amended to become the Every Student Succeeds Act. Among other changes, the law now gives states more control on how schools are evaluated and what steps are required when improvement is deemed necessary. The once-a-year test is still the biggest measure used.

Teacher evaluations are also linked with student performance in many districts. (Imagine your job depending on the results of a once-a-year test given to someone else, let alone children.) Unfortunately, that added stress alone won't change the number of Washington State students failing to meet standards in mathematics, which has ranged from about 20 percent to 50 percent of students, depending on the grade level, over the last several years.[9]

Simply articulating learning standards and implementing accountability measures (i.e., tests) doesn't result in more students learning—just like a new textbook alone won't make students better readers or mathematicians. And while many think high test scores once a year are a good thing, these results often come at a high price.

Test Stress

"Test on Friday" is a statement that many students for years have dreaded. Throughout my years of teaching, I heard the questions: "Do we have to remember this?" and "Is it on the test?" countless times.

Measuring student knowledge and abilities is complicated. Multiple assessments are necessary to determine what students know and what they are capable of. Standardized tests are just one of those measurements and do give some useful information, but no one test—no matter how thorough it is—can give a complete picture of a student's knowledge and abilities; yet we act like it can. The increased anxiety over testing results has risen to the point where the annual test creates a lot of frenzy in schools. Educators at all levels spend countless hours talking about and preparing for the test (remember the test academies?). Unfortunately for students, adults are so stressed about what happens once a year that their common sense often seems to fade.

All sorts of negative, borderline-ridiculous things happen because of the importance placed on the annual test. Starting in September, teachers tell students that what they are learning is on the big test in April—and they had better know it. To an eight-year-old third grader, a test that is seven months away might as well be in a different lifetime. Reminding students about the test at every turn does nothing but cause tremendous anxiety or total apathy. Even worse is that knowledge starts to become something accumulated only for a test—and no other reason. Thus, many students (and adults) believe the school year is over and "check out" after the test when there are still several weeks left.

Before the test, letters are sent home to parents telling them to be sure their child is well-rested, well-nourished, and on-time to school. Not only is it condescending to parents to state the obvious, children need food and sleep, but the letter also implies that this is *the* crucial time to be punctual and the other 170-some-odd school days are not as important.

Teachers are under pressure from principals, who are under pressure from district administrators, who are under pressure from the superintendent, who is under pressure from the school board to ensure students achieve high results on the test—and everyone, including parents and students, feels the pressure of the media and public opinion. It's tough for many students to find the joy in learning in that kind of environment. Clear thinking is difficult enough for, say, a fifteen-year-old under the best of circumstances (like, you have no acne and your friends like you today), let alone after months of being warned about the test and how it is tied to graduation from high school and your whole future.

Often students in middle and high school who did not meet standard on their previous year's mathematics or reading test are required to take a second math or language arts class instead of electives like music, drama, or a foreign language. The second class may or may not be taught in a similar way to what was taught before—a way that obviously did not work for those students to begin with. Plus, electives are not just wasted hours; they are often the highlight of a student's day and frequently are the main motivation for a child making it to school on any given day. How likely is it that a student's test scores are going to improve if you take away their one source of pleasure, motivation, and interest at school? Another aspect to consider is that electives can improve test scores in other areas, if the appropriate content connections are made.

Once, I even observed a middle school holding test pep rallies for large groups of seventh and eighth graders. Adults attempted to encourage the students: "We believe in you!" "You can do it." "Get good sleep and show up on time." The students required to attend that event just happened to be performing in the bottom third of their class. At least 80 percent were children of color. If you were an academically struggling fourteen-year-old Mexican American, would a twenty-minute gathering in the gym help you solve problems on a math test?

I got through the yearly test frenzy by doing the opposite of what many teachers and administrators did: I tried to avoid putting life-or-death-like pressure on the students. I would remind them often that puppies are still cute and ice cream still tastes good no matter what happens on the test. I also strived to align their daily classroom experiences with what they would encounter on the test: teaching to the standards that would be measured and having students practice showing how they arrived at their answers. For example, when I taught eighth-grade math, we did problem-solving as our warm-up every day before diving into the daily lesson. I required the students to show how they solved the problem with words, numbers, or pictures just like they were required to do on the state mathematics test. Doing this not only gave me insight into their understanding but also helped lessen the intimidation factor of the assessments—when test time rolled around, students were not taken aback by what they were asked to do because they had been doing it every day. My students tended to achieve results that were higher than their peers in other classes. To me, though, the best reinforcement was hearing students say to each other, "That wasn't so bad—it was just like our problems of the day, only way too many of them!"

In a world that often bases success on high quarterly profit margins, test scores have become the "product" of schools. Thus, some people believe teacher effectiveness should be measured by test results. How many other professions are judged by how children ages eight to seventeen perform on a few hours of testing each spring? Teachers and administrators feel such pressure to succeed that there are stories of altering tests and cheating to achieve better results. Educational success has come to mean graphs and charts showing high test results. But those charts won't show how much a child has grown to love reading. They won't show how a child has stumbled upon her calling to be an artist or a scientist. They won't show how a child has learned to successfully manage conflict with his peers. There's so much learning that happens for students that is not assessed by the all-important spring test, so we must ask ourselves—is this obsession with testing *really* what's best for children?

The Devil in the Testing Details

Testing doesn't just fall into place every year. It requires a lot of preparation, logistical problem-solving, and all-around hair pulling and gnashing of teeth, as evident in staff meetings like the following:

The principal and testing coordinator (usually a member of the leadership committee that works with the principal to run the school) were discussing the all-important spring test schedule.

"Here is the schedule for the next two weeks of testing," the principal said. "As you know, all PE and music times are altered. We all need to be flexible and focus on the test."

The testing coordinator continued, "Everyone will be testing from nine until about eleven. Recess will start then. Some students may still need time to finish their test, especially the reading and math problem-solving parts. Bathrooms will be off-limits unless there's an emergency. Send your kids two at a time after the second bell to take care of their business. Remember to send your attendance quickly. If a student shows up at school after testing has started, they will be kept in the office until their class is finished testing.

"The library will have third-grade ELL students. Ms. Williams will proctor. Ms. Emerson, the PE teacher, will have fourth-grade ELL in the cafeteria." The coordinator went on with a laundry list of where testing would take place and who would be monitoring the tests. This exchange occurred before computers were required for tests, which is now the case in some places. However, not all schools have enough computers or the capacity for all students to test at the same time. Thus, many of those schools go through a lot of upheaval just to get students in front of a computer, which they may not be familiar with using at all.

The details of testing are daunting to say the least. Just having hundreds of sharpened pencils and making sure everyone has the correct test booklets takes time and effort, but coordinating the many accommodations that need to be available for students is quite the task. Many of the accommodations are for students in special education and must follow their individual education plan (IEP). For example, the plan may dictate that a child must have an adult read problems aloud or serve as a scribe. Some students who are not in special education also warrant accommodations through what's called a 504 plan (similar to an IEP). For example, they may be allotted additional time to complete a section of the test. Other accommodations just make sense for anyone, like limiting the number of students in one room who are testing and making sure appropriate tools are available, like a reading guide (strip of paper to keep track of which line they are reading) or an approved calculator.

The state gives a window of time, usually about three weeks, to test every student from third grade up. The majority of students spend about one to two hours a day for six to seven days taking the test. (Remember, not every grade takes the same number of tests.) Make-up tests are often necessary when students are absent, so it's important to allot time during the last few days of the testing window for these. Many schools try to test mostly on Tuesdays through Thursdays because absences tend to be lower—and attention spans higher—than they are on Mondays and Fridays.

Food for Thought

Snacks for students during testing are a big deal in some places. Some PTAs go to a lot of trouble to prepare snack bags for each child, sometimes for several hundred children. The snacks are distributed every day of testing. At some places, it was up to the teacher to provide snacks, and to be aware of any allergies. Trail mix, fruit, and granola bars are common. Nutritional values vary.

Every adult who is going to proctor the test must go through training. Schools with lots of students needing accommodations must ensure they have enough adults trained, not always easy to do. Music teachers, PE teachers, librarians, paraprofessionals, and counselors can be found proctoring in all sorts of spaces around schools. The whole atmosphere of a school, not to mention daily routines, is discombobulated during test times.

Mornings are when most of the testing takes place, but the rest of the day is thrown for a loop as well. Recess times may be altered. There may be changes to music, physical education, and library classes (when classroom teachers get planning time). Disruption starts and tensions build even before school when teachers are making sure they have their snacks for the day and do other last-minute preparations.

Once the bell rings, there is a short period of time when there are lots of bodies in motion. Students are moving desks, taking attendance to the office, going to the restroom, sharpening pencils, rifling through backpacks to find their reading books, and walking to different rooms for the test. Teachers are posting signs on doors that say, "QUIET—TESTING." Nervousness abounds. The principal is usually scurrying around, checking on classrooms and dealing with misbehaving or upset children.

Then suddenly the halls are still and quiet. Doors are shut. Every group of students that is testing hears the same thing: "Make sure you have your test book. Please follow along as I read the directions out loud. Everyone open their test books to page . . ."

All this is repeated ten times over the next three weeks.

Testing for the Young Ones

K–2 students do not take the big test, but their teachers formally assess them all the time. There are many individual measures given one-on-one. It is challenging to assess one child at a time while a couple dozen five- to seven-year-olds are working "independently."

Most of the students are able to complete that day's test in the allocated time. Many finish with plenty of time to spare. Often, though, a couple of students are slower than the rest of the group and take every last second to finish. (More time is available to any student who needs it.)

It is difficult for a nine-year-old fourth grader to sit still for forty-five minutes while taking the test, and then to remain there, quiet, waiting for everyone to finish. Recess can't come too soon—or at least a grunt and a stretch. Many children are able to read, draw (though that can lead to disruptions like rifling through desks to find colored pencils or borrowing markers), or just lay their heads down and rest.

The tension during test time certainly affects recess as well. The screaming and shouting are a notch or two louder. Tempers of students and adults are shorter. Power struggles are much more frequent outside. Behavior infractions increase, and the principal deals with more discipline issues. And we just accept this.

The quiet of test time is contrasted by the raucous conversations that build up quickly once everyone has turned in their test books. Some teachers like to keep daily lessons going, especially math and reading. Others feel it is a time to relax a bit, with activities such as art.

As an instructional math coach, I helped proctor the spring test in elementary schools and was privy to some interesting post-test conversations in the staff room, like this one:

"I had a couple of students finish in ten minutes today. I made them go back and check each problem," said Ms. Sanford, a young fourth-grade teacher with only a few years of teaching experience.

"Everything went smoothly for me," said Ms. Kiel-Watson, a third-grade teacher, also quite young. "Though a few were squirming in their seats the entire time."

"Did you hear what happened in Ms. Hightower's class? One student started crying when he tore his booklet by erasing so much. He asked if that meant he flunked. Poor guy," Ms. Sanford said.

"Did you notice how easy the computation was? I know we aren't supposed to look at it, but I did," interjected Mr. Schwartz, a fifth-grade teacher, with a sly smile. He was the only male teacher with about ten years' experience.

"I only saw a couple of problems on geometry—we spent five weeks on that unit. What a waste," Ms. Villman, a third-grade teacher who had been teaching for over twenty-five years, coldly stated.

"Science was really hard for them," said Ms. Owens, the other fifth-grade teacher, while shaking her head. "There were beads of sweat on a couple of foreheads. We had only two science kits this year because of time. Scores are going to be bad."

"But science doesn't count towards AYP. We've been told over and over math is the priority. So that's all I care about," Mr. Schwartz said tersely.

"I'm so glad this will be over next week. Then I can finally do what I want," sighed Ms. Villman, with nods of agreement from all.

While listening, I was thinking: (1) this is sad to hear how students are stressing out; (2) the test academies did not seem to help with stress; and (3) I am also looking forward to the end of testing so learning and teaching can be the focus of my work, not testing.

Once testing is complete, you can almost hear the sighs of relief emanating from every school. Both teachers and students begin counting down to the end of the year. A field trip or two might be planned, and you might even see an art project being worked on. Most everyone is fatigued, and conversations about summer plans increase.

No Downtime

An interesting positive aspect of the rigid textbook programs is that to keep pace, teachers need to keep teaching lessons till the end of the school year; they can't just kick back and do whatever after testing. However, many teachers do consider the year over once the big test has passed, and fidelity to programs varies from strict adherence to teaching whatever they like.

Misuse and Misunderstanding of Assessment

By now, you might be thinking, *Wow—this guy thinks testing is the worst thing in the world*. But that's not true. Testing in general gets a bad rap—especially the spring test, which has become high stakes. However, it is not the test itself that is bad; it is actually sound. The problem is what is *done* with the results. There is much misunderstanding about what test results actually indicate, which culminates in administrators misusing data to make decisions.

For example, way too much significance is given to subscores. In mathematics, there is an overall score and several subscores for particular categories like probability and statistics, geometry, or number sense. More than once over my teaching career, I heard administrators cite a low subscore as a reason to put more energy into a particular area of mathematics. For example, if they saw that only 42 percent of fifth-grade students met standard in the geometry section, suddenly everyone had to focus more instructional time on geometry, which means some other topic area was eliminated. Administrators often did not take into consideration that there were only four questions that made up that subscore. Such a paltry number of questions doesn't provide enough data upon which to base huge instructional decisions. While a low subscore does warrant further examination, it, alone, should *not* be the reason for making instructional changes.

Another point to consider is that the test is often administered when there is still a quarter of the year left, yet the standards are year-end. A lot of learning can happen in the last several weeks of a school year that may not be demonstrated on the test. Some places are delaying the big tests until later in the school year for that reason, yet instructional time that occurs after testing is still not taken into account when looking at test data.

Another problem is that way too much emphasis is placed on this one measurement. The best any test can offer is a snapshot of what students can do at a particular time. The test does not give information about why students achieved a certain score; thus, making decisions based only on those test scores can be misguided. Mathematics test results in particular should be examined carefully because the mathematics portion of the test includes word problems. Low scores can indicate that reading skills—rather than computational skills—need work. If we are to make thoughtful, informed decisions about student achievement, then we must use the assessment data we have in a more responsible way—and seek out more sources of data than what is provided on a once-a-year test.

If All Our Ducks Were in a Row

What happens in the classroom regularly should mirror the types of content, contexts, and cognitive demand found in the assessments. That is a major part of curriculum alignment. Have you ever taken a test that covered material not presented in class (at least the one you had been going to), asked you to apply skills to a situation out of left field, or asked you to use skills in a way you were unfamiliar with? Did you start to sweat? Swear under your breath? I know I did!

Are we teaching to the test or to the standards? This is a controversial question, especially among teachers. Teachers complain, and legitimately so, about how "all we are asked to do is teach to the test. That is wrong." A lot of that backlash comes from too much pressure on the one spring test and misunderstanding of the results. However, the test should be aligned with what happens in the classroom on a daily basis. Both tests and classroom instruction should be based upon the standards for that subject and grade level. (The match does seem obvious.) If students' experiences in the classroom every day match the content, context, and cognitive demand expressed in the standards, and the assessment is also aligned, then you have a more accurate measure of learning—and the test is likely to induce much less anxiety for everyone.

Another problem with testing stems from administrators' desire to predict how students will do on the assessments. Several districts require teachers to administer multiple measures prior to the big test that indicate how students are likely to do. Though it could be argued that these measures can indicate the areas where students need more instruction, the effectiveness of the policy is questionable—so much time spent testing hampers teachers' ability to teach. If teachers were trusted to teach to the standards that are measured, then this wouldn't be necessary. With that approach, teachers could show other evidence, like daily work or projects, to demonstrate student learning according to standards. Alignment between what happens in class and what is measured is, again, key.

Focusing only on assessments and testing doesn't allow for enough teaching time. If you don't feed the pig, it won't get heavier simply by weighing it more. In 2014–15, the frustration level of teachers, parents, and students in several Seattle Public Schools got so high with some district-mandated assessments that they refused to give them or opted out of taking them altogether.[10] The controversy over testing is very distracting and not conducive to a positive learning community.

The misunderstanding of assessment data, along with a society that relies on quarterly profit margins to determine success, puts an inordinate amount of importance on annual tests. But it's wrong to treat children as if they are factory parts and to look only at the short-term measures to judge teachers and schools. Children are unique individuals who grow at various rates. Many of us remember a time when we finally blossomed. The progression is not a straight line. Yet we expect steady upward movement for "the bottom line," (i.e., test scores). Unfortunately, many educators forget that test results will improve with authentic learning experiences aligned with the desired standards being measured.

Grades Are Also Assessment Results

Amid all the hoopla about yearly standardized tests, it is easy to forget that grades on report cards are also a form of assessment.

Grading procedures have changed since the early 2000s as districts continue to adopt standards-based learning goals. Most districts have abandoned letter grades of A–F in favor of a number grading system based on specific standards (there may be slight variations on language between districts):

- 1: Exceeding Standard

- 2: Meeting Standard

- 3: Approaching Standard

- 4: Below Standard

Number grades based on specific standards are designed to provide more clarity about what a student is able to do. For example, instead of just receiving a 1 in "Reading," a student might receive a 1 in the category of "Reads grade-level text," and a 2 for "Comprehends main ideas and supporting details."

However, one big grading issue that still remains is how individual teachers decide what grade a student has earned. The huge differences in what teachers determine a particular letter grade means are part of why standards-based systems were developed (though, there has been specific criteria for students at each grade). For example, teachers have been known to give extra credit for actions like donating canned goods to a food drive or wearing school colors on game day. An A student from one class may or may not have the same basic skills and knowledge as an A student from a neighboring class or another school. (So, in some ways, teachers themselves are also to blame for the testing fever). Thus, grading on specific standards has been emphasized.

Grades: My Approach Evolved

When I was growing up and during my first several years of teaching, students earned letter grades. When the switch to standards-based grading came along, it was difficult for many teachers to grasp. Along with several colleagues, I attended a workshop for sixth-grade teachers to better understand the grading system and how to use it. Conducted by a middle school math teacher, the workshop was part of an effort to build understanding and enhance communication between middle and elementary schools, hopefully making the transition easier for students. (One of the big leaps a child makes is from the relatively safe, orderly environment of elementary school to the organized chaos of middle school with roaming mobs of hormonally unbalanced teens and preteens.)

The workshop presenter explained that while the number-based system was helpful, it didn't make sense to the students, so she gave names to each of the different levels (1–4) and used the first letter of each level as the "grade" for each test or assignment:

- 1: Exceeding Standard/Excellent: Grade E

- 2: Meeting Standard/Quality: Grade Q

- 3: Approaching Standard/In Development: Grade I

- 4: Below Standard/Redo (or Revise): Grade R

"I always encourage students to correct their mistakes, especially on I and R papers," the presenter said. "And then give them higher scores if they make the corrections."

One of the teachers asked, "But isn't that letting them cheat? They can just copy the answers from someone else who got it right."

"Oh, that is a real possibility," the presenter said. "But if that's what they are doing, then they will continue to have the same problems. The hope is by correcting their mistakes, they won't make them again. I don't want the kids to just chuck their papers and go, 'Oh well.' I want them to learn, not to punish them for getting wrong answers. If the same errors come up, I will talk to the student and see if I can help them. But I want them to help themselves first."

I liked what was presented, especially how assessing student learning was not just about getting a grade. It was a way to give informative feedback with an emphasis on learning. Giving credit for correcting errors made sense to me then and still does now.

Even with standards, grading is not as consistent as hoped. Teacher judgment is still a factor. Again it brings us back to test scores as a supposedly fair measurement of a student's knowledge and skills. If implemented and interpreted appropriately, data from tests are an informative part of assessing student learning.

If the instructional resources (e.g., textbooks) used by teachers were aligned with the standards and test, as described earlier, then the test just becomes something that happens and changes the schedule some. It isn't as big of a shock to take a test that has similar problems and situations to what you have been dealing with for months. But the driving force behind the test and what goes on daily in the classroom should be the standards themselves, which is not currently the case. There is much work to be done for the sake of all children—less drama and obsession over standardized tests and more understanding about assessments, for starters.

Educators—in particular leadership, which includes principals and district administrators—should be well-versed in measuring student knowledge and abilities, testing being a big part of that measurement. How administration at any level—state, district, or building—looks at and reacts to testing influences students' journeys.

Chapter 5

Leadership: Who Is in Charge?

Leaders Set the Tone

What qualities make a good leader?

I can't answer this question without thinking of Ms. Lawrence (Susan to her staff). When I transferred to her school, I was slated to teach in a portable outside the main building.

"I'm sorry, but the portable is the only room available," Susan said.

I didn't care so much about the portable. I was just happy to be there teaching sixth grade. (I had been teaching fifth grade at my previous school and was looking forward to the change.) Plus, I had heard good things about Susan's style of leadership, though the poverty rate of this school (65–80 percent depending on the year) made for tough conditions.

"Let me know what you need to get settled in," Susan said. "I want to hear more about how you use the newspaper in class. It sounds great."

We went on to have a meaningful discussion about different ways to engage reluctant learners as well as the enthusiastic ones. I would discover that Susan had genuine relationships with staff members, students, and parents. She was one of those rare people of authority—

responsible for a community of over 550 people ranging from ages five to sixty-five—who everyone loved to be around yet dreaded being sent to for reprimands. Even the "frequent flyers" liked her when they weren't in trouble. No one wanted to disappoint her. She was so focused on the welfare of the children above all else, as well as the staff, that the school was an inspiring place to be, even in trying circumstances.

Susan was adamant that every child was capable of learning. She listened, made fair decisions, had a sense of humor, and kept a positive attitude, which was contagious among staff. Teachers wanted to be there to contribute to the positive learning community that she established; she made it clear she understood what it took to teach and that her staff had lives outside of school, yet she never wavered on student learning being the main focus.

Another principal that stood out as an exceptional leader I didn't work for but heard give a presentation at a conference about how she shook up a high school in Texas. It was one of the lowest-performing high schools in Houston; it had a high poverty rate, a high dropout rate, and almost 90 percent of the students were not meeting standard in mathematics. New to that school, she walked in and said she would raise performance so that over 90 percent would meet standard. The other educators at the school laughed at her, and the phrase "When pigs fly!" was tossed around.

She believed one of the issues was that too many students were just slipping through the cracks, dropping out and certainly not achieving academic success. A contributing factor was lack of personal support. So with the help of the curriculum director, she reorganized schedules so that there was time for each student to meet with a caring adult for extra help and attention.

She believed that the struggling students should be working with the most qualified teachers—starting with her! She tutored the toughest five students, brought from juvenile detention each day, and three of them graduated. After four years, more than 90 percent of the students were meeting standard in mathematics. Her staff gave her a plastic pig over two feet long with wings, showing that, indeed, pigs can fly!

Like Susan, this principal was focused on student learning. Both leaders were skilled at motivating people because they had high expectations, for themselves and others. They walked their talk—not only by putting in long hours but filling those hours with activities that fostered meaningful connection, working one-on-one with students, and being visible throughout the day in halls and classrooms. They acknowledged hard work and celebrated the achievements of adults and children. Both leaders brought out the best in students and staff, in part because they had a genuine passion for education and a belief that all children can learn. These are the kind of leaders that create positive learning communities.

Leadership in public schools—and the responsibility of fostering the type of learning communities described in the preceding examples—doesn't begin and end with principals. There are many people at various levels of the system—mostly administrators but some non-administrators as well, like counselors and librarians. School boards and superintendents wield the most control, relying on district administrators like assistant superintendents (often in charge of principals), curriculum directors, staff development coordinators, and budget managers to help carry out directives and policies. Principals are the lead administrators in schools, who in turn rely on vice principals and work with department chairs and teacher leaders to ensure plans are implemented. All levels of leadership, regardless of decision-making power, have influence on student experiences and learning.

How well an administration works with teachers, support staff, students, and parents is all over the board. Relationships range from the dysfunctional—total mistrust and conflict—to highly functional, cooperative, almost kumbaya-like situations. Leaders create the atmosphere at a school, which affects how well they operate. Principals, in particular, can foster a vibrant place where teaching and learning are the focus, or they can create a stressful environment where test scores, straight lines, and strict rules are emphasized. In which place would you rather be?

Unfocused Leadership

Often how smoothly a school year begins is a reflection of leadership. One year in early August when I was working as an instructional coach, I attended a leadership committee meeting, the first one, with the principal, the vice principal, and a teacher with leadership duties.

We had gathered to discuss the coming August workshop, and so far, stress was squashing the positive.

The principal, Ms. Rayburn, had been at the school for seven years. She'd started out as a special education teacher and was a fairly intense woman who wanted the best for all students, which wasn't easy to deliver; it was a diverse school with over 70 percent of the students qualifying for reduced or free lunch.

As the meeting began, Ms. Rayburn looked up from her notepad and, with a slight edge to her voice, said, "We have to make sure everyone is on board with the positive discipline policy. The discipline committee will be making a presentation. The playground supervisors will need to be on board and not write up so many kids. They will need help teaching the students how to play at recess. We have to have that in place from the get-go. The teachers will need to be held accountable for the fidelity of how they teach reading. They'll need help getting their reading materials together, so someone needs to be assigned to that. I will go over the test scores from last year. The teachers aren't going to be happy." Here, I wondered if she was going to take a breath. "We have to get ready for the open house and make sure teachers get help organizing their talks because it's also our curriculum night. It has to be structured. Oh, and the teachers will really need some help with conferences in October so we will have to plan for that. Who's dealing with lunch on the workshop day for the new math program? How's that day going to be structured? We need to have all this worked out."

After a brief moment, I asked, "So what's the priority?"

"It's all a priority!" Ms. Rayburn said.

There was a pause filled with awkward glances among the group.

The vice principal, with a puzzled look, asked, "What needs to be done first?"

"Everything."

Another pause. I was thinking, sarcastically, *Ah the joy of a new year!*

There are usually certain elements present in August meetings, one being the goal of a positive attitude and hope for the year. Some leaders convey this better than others. How administration looks at the challenges of their positions can motivate others or cause tension.

Most schools have some sort of all-staff meeting, like what we were planning in the awkward situation with Ms. Rayburn, before the school year begins. Administrators spend a lot of time planning those meetings, which can last anywhere from two to six hours. The agendas are a mix of mandated items—like discussion about new textbooks or updates about new policies and programs—and items of choice by the principal, like how to make the playground safer or how to get more parents volunteering with the PTA. These meetings present an opportunity for principals to establish their priorities for the school year and nurture the atmosphere for the staff.

Even with the best intentions, which is usually the case, some administrators, like Ms. Rayburn, do not bring decisive leadership or create vibrant learning communities. Staying focused and engaging in calm decision-making are key ingredients of effective leadership. In the absence of that, staff and students are less likely to feel motivated, and without their buy-in, it's tough to get anything accomplished.

Shared Leadership through Committees

There are many complex, often invisible facets involved in educating groups of children. While textbooks and testing tend to be the main focus of the media, there are many other areas of concern for school administration: providing instructional leadership for all subjects and grades; creating a safe place for hundreds of children and dozens of adults to work and learn in every day; managing teachers, custodians, office staff, bus drivers, food workers, day-care operators; and handling traffic flow in the mornings and afternoons (quite the adventure at some schools—sometimes adults are worse at following rules than children). Principals are ultimately responsible for everything that happens in a school, and superintendents are responsible for everything that happens in a district. Yet all these responsibilities are too much for one person to handle alone. Principals and superintendents delegate many tasks to committees populated by teachers and other staff.

Committees are usually filled before the school year officially starts. "Make sure you sign up for at least one committee before we take our break today" is a typical statement heard at August all-staff meetings. The excitement of a new year makes it a little easier to get people to volunteer.

District and Building-Level Committees

The most common committees are district-wide and focus on a particular subject area, like science, mathematics, reading, or social studies. With representatives from each school in the district, these committees facilitate communication between district administration and classroom teachers, especially when there are new standards or tests. These committees also sometimes take on other tasks like piloting new textbooks or developing supplemental resources for classrooms. There are also subject-specific committees for specialists like teachers of physical education, music, library science, and special education.

Middle and High School Committees

Middle and high schools have different needs, so their committee work is structured differently. They predominately have department heads that conduct meetings with teachers from the same school in their subject area. Those department heads then go to district meetings with other department heads.

Other committees are specific to each school, also known as building-level committees. These can include social committees (a.k.a. the party-planning, morale-boosting "Aren't we all happy now!" committee), discipline committees, emergency/safety committees, and some sort of a leadership team.

While committees are intended to encourage communication, they can easily end up spinning their wheels to no more effect than the hamster in the class cage. In my experience, most committee participation was a waste of time, and I think it's safe to say that I'm not alone. For example, a committee was once tasked with creating a new mission statement for their school. Within a few months of doing so, almost everyone forgot about it and yet at least a hundred hours had been put into crafting it and arguing over semantics. In another example, a committee argued for over six hours about criteria for making the honor roll and about what the honor roll bumper sticker should look like. The stickers—and the criteria—were only used for two years. It can be frustrating for teachers and staff to spend hours on an issue, make a decision (finally), have it implemented (mostly), and then see it abandoned after a brief time, or even have it completely ignored.

Many schools require every certified teacher to be on at least one committee (part of the "other duties as necessary" listed in the union contract). Since these "other duties" do not typically pay any extra money, people understandably tend to sign up for committees that require the least amount of extra work and time commitment. Thus the social committee and emergency/safety committee tend to fill up first since they typically meet only a few times each school year.

Subject-specific and other district-level committees usually meet only once a month. But when you add in regular staff meetings, plus grade-level or department meetings, suddenly some teachers have to attend between one and three meetings each week after long days in the classroom. In my experience, these meetings were most often held between 4:30 and 7:00 p.m. and were not the most productive (especially the last hour). Teachers with children of their own often had to leave early or not attend, sadly limiting their input and somewhat defeating the purpose of shared leadership. Committee participation involves sinking significant effort and time into projects that may or may not make a positive difference in student learning. Is it worth it?

Leadership Teams

Leadership teams, one type of building-level committee, meet more often than subject-specific committees and have lots of extra tasks. As a result, they are sometimes the hardest to fill. Leadership teams not only serve as the communication link between staff and the principal but are also vital to running a school. For example, principals rely on the leadership team to share information from the district or state with staff, help prepare PowerPoint presentations for staff meetings, plan and facilitate workshops, ensure teachers have enough materials for their classrooms (surprising how many teachers don't respond to email), keep abreast of what the other building-level committees are doing (which are often led by members of the leadership team), and provide doughnuts or other treats at meetings.

So who is it that typically works with principals on leadership teams? In my experience, these teams were usually composed of a classroom teacher or two—preferably one primary level and one intermediate level—the vice principal/head teacher, a paraprofessional, and maybe a counselor. Sometimes a special education teacher, a reading or math specialist, or an ELL teacher will also be on the leadership team. In short, the makeup of leadership teams varies greatly, and unfortunately, the folks on these teams aren't necessarily the most qualified for the work. Due to the significant time commitment involved, a lot of people, sometimes the most capable and respected, refuse to participate. Others will do anything for the extra stipend that sometimes accompanies the position (maybe only $250 a year). There are also the people who are compelled to volunteer because they like to feel important. Thus, participation on the leadership team is not necessarily an indication of the competence or compatibility of participants. Sometimes a principal will have choices, but just as likely they will simply inherit a group. Whatever the mix, this group plays an important role in shaping the school year, starting with planning the August meetings.

For better or worse (probably depending on whom you talk to), I ended up on a few leadership teams throughout the years and therefore helped to plan and execute a number of August workshops. It definitely increased my appreciation for the task. Done well, it takes a lot of work. The district mandates some of the content, and then the leadership team is left to plan the rest. The length of the meetings is typically dictated by funding and union-negotiated contract language about workloads, so often there is either too much crammed in or not enough information to fill the allotted time. Many staff members, myself included, daydreamed of being elsewhere when the time was not productive.

One school I had the pleasure of supporting for a couple of years had a skilled leadership team that was systematically changing the culture of the school's instruction in a positive way. They wanted to decrease the amount of lecture/teacher-dominated discussions to focus more classroom time on student-led inquiry, especially in mathematics.

The team understood that a change of this magnitude would take a while to implement and that incremental steps are necessary for success, similar to how you don't leap from addition straight to calculus. To guide teachers through this process, the team developed a plan to provide support, which is where I came in. As a teacher on special assignment supporting instruction in math and science in over forty schools, I welcomed the opportunity to work with the teachers and leaders of that school. It helped that I had taught with one of the more vocal staff members previously and she respected me. Also, I made it clear that I had no evaluative authority and was only there to help, not judge or "rat on" anyone.

The leadership team knew the process was going to take more than one school year, so they set reasonable goals for each year. The teachers were assigned to review research about student-led inquiry to create a common foundation of knowledge. Then to meet the needs of each teacher, the principal and his leadership team decided who (myself or one of the leadership team members) would work best with whom in terms of providing support. Some teachers were already working toward having students be responsible for their own learning, while others were still doing most of the talking in their classrooms.

The leadership team requested teachers engage in pre-lesson conferences and planning sessions, with me or one of the team members, to set goals and discuss potential problems. The goals for each teacher were different depending on what grade they taught and their comfort level with the student-led inquiry approach. For example, the goal for kindergarten teachers was to get their students to ask each other, "How do you know you are correct?" And then have the students be able to demonstrate this. For the fifth and sixth graders, the goals included asking classmates to please show what they mean, and to either say, "I respectfully disagree because . . ." or "I agree because . . ." with the reasons being most important. Teachers held post-lesson meetings with me or a member of the leadership team to reflect on whether goals were met, what went well, and what didn't.

The principal and his leadership team worked hard to support the teachers throughout this process, while keeping the focus on student learning. They believed in the ability of the students and teachers, and their passion for teaching and learning was contagious. Part of their effectiveness was due to their common ideals of what good instruction should consist of and that they liked each other and their work. The team created a positive environment and fostered genuine relationships among adults, students, and the community. And without focusing on testing at all, student scores on standardized tests improved . . . Imagine that!

Regardless of what kind of committee teachers serve on—leadership or otherwise—you may have come to the realization that has daunted many budding educators and frustrated many veteran teachers: hours and hours are spent on committee tasks not necessarily related to the actual teaching of children. Some of this work is vital to keep schools running, such as planning staff workshops and emergency preparedness (what to do in earthquakes or fires), yet won't help a child learn to read. Still, the behind-the-scenes work is underpublicized and underpraised, and it's a significant part of the daily goings-on for teachers.

Teacher unions and administrations have been discussing teacher workloads for years and years, and there still remains little consensus about what level of time commitment is expected, what tasks outside actual teaching are necessary, and what constitutes fair compensation for all the extra duties teachers are expected to fulfill. Teacher workloads among neighboring districts can vary because each district has their own labor agreement with the teachers union. Sadly, district budget constraints decide a majority of decisions about workloads, rather than what is necessary for student learning.

Another area that is (supposed to be) focused on student learning and also has been a topic of discussion for years between unions and administration is teacher observations.

Observations: Quality "Control"

At an October staff meeting the principal announced, "It's time for the first round of observations. I need to schedule a pre-conference, observation, and post-conference with you all over the next three weeks. The second observation will be in late winter or early spring. For the first one, I want to see a reading lesson. The second one will be math." A mixture of slightly audible gasps, rolling of eyes, and nodding of heads (as if they knew it was coming) followed the announcement. Some teachers stress out about observations, some are just irritated by them, some don't care one way or the other, and some even like them—regardless, everyone has to participate.

Every year, principals are required to schedule formal teacher observations as part of quality control. Unions and districts negotiate the parameters; for example, how many observations occur in a year (usually between one and five), how they are scheduled, whether drop-ins count, the criteria for excellent instruction, and what is to be done with the observations, both good and bad. Sometimes seniority is a factor in the number and format of observations. Teachers new to a district usually have more observations with greater detail than teachers with previous experience within that district. It was interesting for me to be considered a new teacher when I had changed districts voluntarily after thirteen years of successful teaching—this says something about the mistrust between systems.

Usually, a pre-conference is scheduled to discuss the observation and lesson. Some principals will delve into details of lesson plans, while others will just talk about scheduling the observation and post-conference times with maybe a brief glance at lesson plans. I understand why some principals want to see lesson plans written out in detail, but it's a big pain. While it is important for teachers to have a plan and understand the desired learning goal for each lesson, it's more important to focus on how the lesson actually went, not whether it was written out well. Some lousy teaching has come from great lesson plans.

This speaks to the inconsistencies that exist between various principals (and teachers). Different aspects of teaching can be deemed important or not, depending on the administrator. Principals naturally have a huge impact on how a building functions. Among the many challenges and responsibilities, they serve as instructional leaders of teachers who have a range of experience, from zero to thirty-five plus years. How that range of experience is acknowledged and respected, as well as held accountable, is a skill that some principals demonstrate and others do not.

The whole conference process can be stressful for everyone—teachers, principals, and students alike. As a sixth-grade teacher in a teachers' lounge (a place where I often just listened as teachers tend to be talkative around other adults), one day I overheard a conversation that has stuck with me (and I have heard variations of many times):

Ms. Thomas, a fourth-grade teacher with three years of experience, though new to the school, asked, "I have my pre-conference tomorrow. What's it going to be like?"

Ms. Davis, a teacher with twenty-five years' experience and a positive personality, responded, "You have to be on your toes with a couple of things, especially how you introduce the lesson. She [meaning the principal] really harps on that. Don't worry—you're a great teacher."

"I hate observations. They don't help me at all. I just get stressed," added Ms. Longmire, a fifth-grade teacher with six years' experience.

"Just pick an easy lesson and really prepare—that's what I used to do. Then you can go back to normal teaching as soon as she leaves," said Ms. Crossley, a somewhat jaded third-grade teacher with over twenty years of experience. "But I don't care about observations anymore. They can't fire me for one bad lesson."

As I listened to the conversation, I felt grateful not to be the principal and pleased that my observation went fine, though it hadn't been particularly informative. The principal had provided general feedback on what I did, but she didn't say much that helped me grow as a teacher.

"I heard about a teacher who got put on a plan of improvement because of one bad observation. It was a mess. The principal just didn't like her, I think. The teacher filed a grievance," said Ms. Longmire.

"I just do what I normally do. What you see is what you get," added Ms. Crossley with a smirk.

"I hope Jason and Nicole aren't there for my observation tomorrow. They really can mess up a lesson," Ms. Henderson said quietly, a respected first-grade teacher with fifteen years' experience.

"I wish we could be just left alone. She knows I get so nervous. Every time she's in my room, something goes wrong," Ms. Longmire said, shaking her head.

"She doesn't know good teaching," said Ms. Crossley. "She spends the whole time typing on her damn laptop, never looking up."

I left the room thinking, *I'm glad I work with children.*

So, many teachers conduct lessons differently when they are observed. Some get so nervous that they "bribe" their students with candy or extra recess for good behavior. I even once heard of a teacher teaching the lesson the day before and then repeating it for the observation. A lot of the time the lesson is structured with the principal in mind, not the students. That is why some administrators want to drop in unannounced, to see what really happens. Union rules have strict guidelines on what can be used from drop-ins, usually little. But shouldn't a principal be able to see what is going on in a *public* school?

In schools, the intention is that principals and vice principals (especially in middle and high schools) act as instructional leaders, and teacher observations are touted as being part of professional growth. While some teachers have mentioned being reminded of good instructional practices here and there, like waiting an appropriate amount of time for students to respond to questions or moving around the classroom more, I have never heard a teacher say they were better at their job because of formal observations. (However, having an instructional coach who has no evaluative power and collaborates on lessons is another story altogether. This is discussed in Chapter 6.)

Sometimes formal observations are the most contact a teacher has with a principal. Over the years, I worked for a few principals who seemed invisible, which had positives, such as feeling like a trusted professional, and negatives, such as feeling like no one was in charge.

During my observations, I tried to teach in my normal fashion, mostly because I wanted to be professional and conduct myself with integrity, which meant doing things the way I usually did. I also didn't want to show students that I would teach one way with the principal there and another when she was not there. They would know it was phony and that wasn't what I wanted to show them. Also, it is just easier to be who you are.

Over the years, a couple principals gave thoughtful feedback that was tied to pre-observation goals; for example, pointing out that I mixed up the difficulty level of questions during reading or asking whether I was using objects appropriately in mathematics. Most of the time I received a lot of praise, which made me feel good and reinforced the positive practices. Though a couple of times I was a bit defensive from the critical feedback, it was good for me because I would reflect on it later to grow as a teacher.

Throughout my career, I also had three principals who were just no help at all. For example, during the observations two of them focused on recording the timeline of my lessons (10:15—brought students in from recess; 10:17—started directions for handing in homework, etc.). The third principal never looked up from her laptop during observations and then questioned me about things she missed, like did I give a time limit for the students' assignment. I just pointed to where the information was written on the board. Sadly, the time and effort those principals put into observing me did not make a bit of difference in my teaching, creating many a missed opportunity for growth.

Teachers should be held accountable for their teaching, and observing what happens in the classroom is one way of doing that. Principals (and vice principals in middle and high schools) have varied experience themselves in teaching as well as in how to effectively observe and critique teachers. With all the other duties involved in running a school, it is no wonder that teacher observations don't always improve instruction. More collaboration between teacher unions and districts on professional development of teachers and teacher quality could help improve the effectiveness of observing teachers.

Staffing Buildings

In addition to providing instructional leadership, another big facet of the principals' responsibilities is staffing their schools. You might think this isn't such a big deal—you figure out how many teachers you need and you hire them—but principals face a number of constraints when it comes to staffing. Perhaps the biggest constraint is how many teachers they can have on staff, which is dictated by state funding. The state pays each district for the number of teachers allocated, but that number may or may not be enough.

It amazes me how often schools start the year with the wrong number of teachers. Yet figuring out the correct number is complex, especially in areas with high student mobility. Administrators make projections in the spring using certain formulas to determine the number of teachers needed the following school year. However, the number of students that actually show up in the fall may be—and often are—different from the projections. A lot of places use the number of students present on October 1 to serve as the final numbers for that year. Thus, in the first week of October, several classes must be adjusted—new ones added or some canceled—based on those final student counts. Sometimes principals scramble come fall to hire additional teachers or have to transfer a teacher to another building due to inaccurate projections.

This upheaval can be upsetting to many children who have already started to settle into a routine with a particular teacher and group of classmates. It is also not easy for the teachers, especially the ones who have to change schools. Often it feels like you start the year over, yet with a month less to teach, which creates more stress as standards do not change and time to fit in the allotted content is already tight.

One of the reasons teacher staffing is so difficult is the high rate of student mobility, particularly in August and September. And when more students move during the school year, schools must accommodate them. That is why one year I had as many as thirty-two sixth graders, though I had started the year with twenty-seven students. About ten students moved in and out during that school year. Another year in a different building, thirty-six fifth graders showed up with only me allocated to teach that grade. (It was a small school with an extensive special education program.) The solution was to split the students by ability for half the day. Another teacher was hired to teach the top nineteen students half days. I taught the other sixteen more struggling students the core subjects of reading, math, and language arts. In the afternoons, all thirty-six students (it was crowded) were with me for social studies and science.

It took a lot of effort to keep the agenda flowing smoothly during those afternoons. While the children coped well, their learning experience would have been vastly improved had there been fewer of them—I could have given more individual attention, for example, or some students might have spoken up more with fewer classmates in the room. Student mobility is a factor that isn't likely to change, but is there a more efficient way to approach it that doesn't lead to overcrowded classrooms and overburdened teachers? There's no easy answer, but the question should be asked.

In March and April, once the big test is over, administrators start examining enrollment projections to staff for the following year. Rumors and guessing are rampant among teachers. While many want to stay in their jobs, other teachers desire to move on to another school, another grade, another district, or maybe into leadership. There are also the usual life transitions, such as marriage, the birth of children, or spouse job changes, that lead to turnover. Though teachers' jobs are more secure than others (thanks to strong unions), budget cuts and threats of layoffs are fairly common.

Staffing of buildings and districts is a key responsibility of administration. Principals cannot change their budgetary allocations from the state, but they can model how to handle changes that are out of their control, hopefully by exhibiting grace and focusing on solutions. I don't know how to improve the projection process, but key considerations as part of a review of public education are appropriate class size, how funds are allocated from the state, and how big schools should be. Of course, keeping optimal student learning is the most important consideration of all.

Hiring, Firing, and the Admin Shuffle

The hiring of teachers and other staff is a major responsibility of leadership. The hiring process in any realm is difficult. What a person puts on their résumé, or what they say in an interview, does not always match what they do in practice. Being able to sense whether a person will be an ideal fit for a position is a skill not all administrators possess.

Successful principals are able to hire people who will work together to create schools where students learn, thrive, and grow. While administrators attempt to hire people that will best fit the system in their school (for example, those who believe that strict adherence to textbooks is crucial to student learning) and are the most capable for their jobs, there is a wide range of effectiveness among teachers, as pointed out in Chapter 3. (Remember some of the discrepancy is due to the inconsistencies in teacher preparation programs. Each university has its own requirements, and the coursework also varies between institutions—some places focus more on theory, while others emphasize methods, for example.)

One of the problems new teachers face is a disconnect between their student teaching placement and where they get a job. For example, the competition for teaching jobs in the Puget Sound area has always been high (special education, math, and science being the exception); thus, many new teachers take whatever they can get for work, often jobs in highly diverse, urban schools. I observed many new teachers struggling with the diversity in their classrooms, in part because their internships had been in schools with student bodies that were mostly white and of a high socioeconomic status. Those types of schools are predominately where many teachers went to school themselves, and therefore within their comfort zones.

Well over half of public-school teachers in the Puget Sound area are white women of middle- to upper-class backgrounds, which mirrors teacher demographic trends across the United States.[11] One course on multicultural education doesn't adequately prepare teachers for the realities of working in schools that are racially and economically diverse. When these teachers get hired in these kinds of schools, they experience culture shock and face difficulties in the classroom for which they are not prepared, like working with students from foreign countries, managing larger class sizes, or teaching students who do not have computers at home.

This disconnect between teachers' training experiences and the realities of the job contributes to staff development issues, along with questions about hiring processes. If teachers aren't prepared for where they teach, how do they get hired in the first place? The application process, as in a lot of professions, is daunting and wrought with problems. Some applications ask for extensive written responses to questions, and while there is some overlap between applications in different districts, there is enough of a difference for a need to rewrite every response. For example, "State briefly what and how you can contribute to this school" is similar to "What do you think would be your major accomplishment in your first five years with X School District?" Also, "Describe the instructional strategies you find to be the most effective for increasing student achievement, particularly with at-risk students" is similar to "With which students do you feel you could be most effective? Explain."

While answers to these questions can demonstrate good writing and reasoning skills, they don't tell you how effective someone is in front of thirty children. District interviewers have certain phrases and terms that they look for and can get fooled by eloquently worded responses. Prospective teachers who may be highly skilled at actually working with children day in and day out may not even make it to an interview if they don't express themselves well in applications or cover letters, or use the proper educational buzzwords.

The applicants who do make it past this first round of screening experience a variety of interview styles and settings that aren't always effective. Sometimes the interview is a relaxed conversation with the principal and maybe one or two other people. Other times, an interviewee might sit before an uptight panel of eight educators asking a dozen form questions.

In more formal interviews, the same questions are usually posed to each candidate and the interviewers take notes about the responses. Over the years, I noticed some interviewers had a way of engaging a candidate and making eye contact as they took notes, while others were so mechanical, so busy furiously writing, I wondered if they were really present. Often the interviewers are looking for key terms and elements in candidate responses, like "differentiation" (a current buzzword that means teaching to meet the specific needs of individual learners with diverse learning needs in a class) or the importance of positive discipline.

Each question is scored on some kind of scale, where points are earned by using certain terms. Sometimes the interviewee with the highest score gets the job, and other times (though not openly) the person who the interviewers want for the position gets it, regardless of the score. The problem is, how well a person performs in an interview doesn't necessarily indicate how good of a teacher that person is. (Can any interview really predict how well a person will perform their job?)

It is only in action that one can really see who can teach. Once, when I applied for a middle school mathematics position, I had to teach a mini-lesson to my three interviewers with about five minutes to prepare. It is the only time I had to demonstrate a lesson during an interview (and over the years I had many interviews, especially when I was first certified). It seems like a useful way of finding out whether a teacher can actually teach.

In the absence of seeing a potential hire in action, recommendations carry a lot of weight. If the screeners are familiar with the person providing the recommendation, it could be good or bad for the candidate, depending on how they feel about this person. Also, the actual content of the letter is important—as is what's *not* in the letter. Again, the screeners may be looking for specific items, like if the applicant is adept at parent communication, has experience with demographics similar to the school being applied to, or has received training in a certain program.

Often the intent is to hire someone who best fits the school culture, a person who will be compliant with administration and not make waves. Yet that person may not be the best fit for the students. There are a lot of rules about fairness in hiring, yet I wonder sometimes how certain people get positions.

Some of the movement of seasoned teachers and administrators is also a concern. Union rules and contracts make it difficult and time-consuming to fire someone. Instead, the solution is often to put extra effort into supporting them, or they are simply moved to a position likely to be a better fit or where they cause the least harm, like moving a sixth-grade teacher to second grade because the younger students are not tested or moving a principal from a dysfunctional school to one that is doing well (high test scores and happy parents) and hoping for the best. Some superintendents believe that principals should move every two to four years no matter what. It always intrigued me how Puget Sound school districts seemed to exchange district-level administrators and principals. The shuffling of school leaders to hopefully make up for the ones who are not getting desired results seems wrong. If a principal has been leading a school for four years and it is working well, disrupting the whole community just because doesn't make sense.

Turnover among other leadership positions is also common. For example, a special education director or curriculum director stays a few years in one district, tries to improve things (remember the complexity of reform), then goes on to a different district to repeat the process. Politics within districts seemed to play a part in who would get leadership positions and be able to keep them.

Any organization will usually function better if all personnel are working together toward the same goal and have common beliefs about how they should conduct their business. Education is the same. Schools where the staff all share a common belief in what quality education is and how a school should function, like how discipline should be handled or how lessons should be taught, will tend to have more success than places where adults don't have a common foundation. Hiring the right people is thus a necessity. That is one of the many challenges of leadership. Some places, usually the larger systems, are more formulaic in their approaches, which is understandable for fairness. Yet I appreciated the interviews where follow-up questions were allowed and it was more of a conversation than just answering canned questions. I also believe teachers should somehow be asked to demonstrate teaching—as nerve-racking as that can be (yet no more than preparing for questions in front of a panel). Who leadership hires can make or break the effectiveness of any part of public education.

New Mandates

Besides who they hire, district leaders make decisions that affect students and teachers through mandates: new ideas and plans for how to improve schools. Some are related to students, like introducing new discipline policies, while others are about instituting dress codes for teachers (probably not the most meaningful use of time and resources). New mandates tend to garner sighs and snickers from teaching staff because they change every three to five years. It's common to hear a statement like "Just when the students really get how the new discipline policies work, they say we have to follow this new procedure and use completely different vocabulary!"

As mentioned in Chapter 1, new mandates sometimes begin with an administrator who was inspired by a session at a conference and returned to school saying, "This is what we should be doing!" Unfortunately, the execution of ideas can get skewed, misused, and create a lot of havoc.

One example was a district that put many resources into getting teachers to plan their lessons according to a certain format. (I have actually seen several different movements in this area. Some places will hire people only with training in certain lesson-planning formats and methods.) For three years, the district paid "experts" to conduct mandatory workshops on yearlong planning, unit planning, and lesson planning. Form rather than actual function was so emphasized that what happened on paper mattered more than how teachers and students actually worked together.

Many teachers, including myself, felt negatively about this mandate and therefore produced the bare minimum of paperwork to cover our behinds, but still we taught in the way we always did. In hindsight, the idea of good planning is important and the format we learned about had beneficial elements. Yet proper planning is only part of good teaching, not an end-all guarantee. "If all our teachers would plan their lessons and units well, then test scores will go up" was a statement I frequently heard. Yet the lessons still need to be taught, and life rarely goes exactly according to plan—especially when dealing with groups of children.

Another district was focused on the idea of making administration walk-throughs more meaningful after one central office administrator attended a workshop at a conference on that topic. With only so many hours in the day, the amount of time an administrator can spend in any one classroom is limited. Thus administrators may do a five-minute walk-through of a class and jump to many conclusions. Another issue is that administrators are all over the board with what they want to see in a class, perhaps that the day's schedule is easily visible or student work is displayed.

One particular district created a checklist of specific elements to look for during walk-throughs. The creator of the system presented different aspects that were touted to help teachers and schools be more consistent and clear with expectations, as well as how a lesson would flow. One aspect of the program was to have three questions visible and discussed for every lesson at all grades: (1) What are the students learning? (2) Why are they learning it? (3) How will it be used in life? Understandable for some lessons and some grades, but trying to get a nine-year-old to articulate how identifying a verb will be used in a science career is just silly. (A more immediate reason for an activity or lesson is more meaningful to a young child.)

This approach was in part a reaction to a common comment heard from high school students: "When will I ever use this? It won't help me be a better ____." Fill in the blank. Or the many adults who can be heard saying, "I've never used most of the crap I learned in high school." While that may be true, the point of many lessons in school is to exercise the brain and practice problem-solving, not necessarily ensure students incorporate concepts like the Krebs cycle into their careers. Knowing why you are learning something is valid, but the reason could be as simple as "learning how to summarize what you have read will help you in class today, tomorrow, in school for the next ___ years, and in your career for the rest of your life."

Suddenly it became a huge deal to have those three things displayed and talked about for every lesson, because administration would look for it right off the bat and maybe even ask a student if they knew what they were learning and how it would be useful. Knowing the answer to those three questions became more important than the lesson itself, and while many teachers made it meaningful and didn't spend a bunch of time stewing about it, many considered it a worthless hoop they had to jump through just to please administration. Their attitude was no secret and students could sense it. Sadly, it also showed how many teachers couldn't even identify the goal of lessons. From what I observed, the positive impact on student learning was minimal and a lot of teachers rebelled against it.

Focus on the 60 Percent

It is a challenge to introduce any new concept to a large group of people. In general, about 20 percent will buy in to the new thing because it is new, and about 20 percent will refuse because it is new (usually a threat to their ego, making them think what they have been doing is wrong, which may or may not be the case). The other 60 percent are the ones who need convincing.

But not all new mandates are ineffective—some can be positive. For example, a local Seattle district had a mandate about how adults talk to each other. They believed strongly in having structure for their conversations so they could be more productive and give everyone a voice. The structure basically reinforced common courtesies of listening, not judging, and allowing for differences of opinions. All personnel, from the superintendent to custodians, practiced paraphrasing and using accepting language (basically validating the other person's thoughts) in all conversations, two important elements of the structure. One result was more collaboration and less grumbling among adults, and interactions with students and parents also became more positive. It is a smaller district that many employees never want to leave. And the students perform in general above state averages.

For many reasons, new mandates—whether helpful or not—seem to go by the wayside after just a few years. Part of the reason is that leadership changes and new leaders bring in their own ideas more often than not. Whatever the reason, the students (who could provide some valuable insights if asked) are the ones most often affected by the policies, without having any say in the matter. Yet if there was more collaboration between classroom teachers, unions, and administration, maybe there would be less resistance to new ideas, and those ideas, if deemed useful, could be sustained over the long haul.

Long Days, Many Hats

It is important to realize that many leadership positions require about seventy-five hours each week just to keep afloat. Principals are supposed to be money managers and instructional leaders for whatever subjects and grade levels are at their particular school. They are expected to attend district meetings—which can take precious time away from the daily goings-on at schools, act as cheerleader and disciplinarian for students and staff, communicate effectively with parents, diffuse volatile situations with students or adults, and manage the mounds of paperwork, including district and state reports and teacher evaluations, and if they are really good, be familiar with each student and their family situation (somewhat impossible at larger schools). Leadership positions are by no means cushy jobs.

The leaders who build trust, are student focused, supportive of teachers, and knowledgeable about the ins and outs of life in actual classrooms are usually better at fostering a positive, functional atmosphere. If administration hires people that have the same core values, the better the chance the adults will like each other and get along, creating a pleasant environment conducive to learning. Students get to see adults working hard and enjoying themselves as well. Or conversely, they get to witness bickering and dissonance, lots of closed doors and tension.

Principals in particular are influential in creating a school culture, either positive or not. The better leaders are the ones who can get the right personnel and create a sense of community with everyone working toward the common goal of student learning. Sometimes, a little luck helps.

Being grounded in beliefs, with actions that support those beliefs, is part of effective leadership. Actions can include providing ongoing meaningful support for staff that fosters their growth. All levels of educators need continuous training to maintain their teaching credentials. The content of their continuing education courses, determined by leadership mostly, is also a factor in what students are taught. If teachers, for example, are required to attend workshops on writing skills or classroom management, that content will inevitably become part of the teachers' practice and is a reflection of what leadership values. Administrators who walk their talk, so to say, can inspire teachers and students.

Chapter 6

Staff Development: What Do Educators Learn?

The School Day's Not Over

It's four o'clock on a Tuesday afternoon in November and forty-two teachers squeeze themselves into chairs meant for ten-year-olds. The heat in this particular room, the only one available for a group of this size, doesn't work. Those who didn't have the foresight to wear their coats are shivering and rubbing their arms. As the presenter for this staff development workshop begins her PowerPoint presentation about strategies for improving mathematics test scores, some teachers are checking email on their phones, some are shifting uncomfortably in their too-small seats, and many are simply lost in their own thoughts:

Do we have milk in the fridge?

I can't feel my toes.

Will this be over in time for me to pick Becky up from soccer practice?

I wish I could sleep with my eyes open.

You can probably guess how much information from the presentation the audience retained, much less implemented into their teaching practice. Yet this is a common staff development scenario in many schools. Helping teachers improve the quality of their teaching is not an easy task. The logistics alone of providing meaningful staff development opportunities (finding enough adult chairs or ensuring the heat works in the room, for example) can be overwhelming. So why bother?

Ideally, when it's done right, staff development for educators transfers to increased student learning. A dynamic, knowledgeable teacher of educators can inspire teachers to try a new instructional strategy, use a different resource, or implement a new discipline policy. Teachers and administrators in Washington State are required to have at least fifteen credit hours (or 150 clock hours) of professional development/ coursework every five years in order to maintain credentials. The amount of credit varies just a little across the nation, from fifteen to twenty quarter credits (or 150–200 clock hours). Clock hours are usually earned from district-run classes, conferences, or state-sponsored workshops. Salaries are also connected to the amount of education beyond a bachelor's degree. Thus, staff development is an integral part of public education, and can take different forms: university courses, district- and school-led courses, coaching, or peer learning.

Clock Hours vs. Tuition

Every ten clock hours (ten hours of class time) is equivalent to one quarter credit hour. Clock hours are much cheaper than paying university tuition, with the cost being about two dollars per clock hour or twenty dollars per credit hour versus about a hundred bucks per credit hour at universities.

University Courses

Perhaps the most well-known type of staff development for educators is university courses, which are typically held during the summer, at night, or on weekends. Often these are taken as part of a master's or doctorate program. Some classes are about pedagogy or focus on specific content areas like social studies or reading. Many teachers choose the courses they want, and these courses may or may not align with what the schools are doing. For example, a teacher may take a course about integrating art into mathematics, which is a great idea in theory, but if the teacher works at a school where the math text needs to be followed with fidelity, then incorporating art in a meaningful way is going to be difficult, perhaps impossible. Taking courses that align with a school's approach to teaching and the use of instructional materials may be a better use of time and resources, but it doesn't always happen that way. This disconnect is sometimes due to new district mandates or teachers changing school. (It's also part of the reason districts and schools conduct their own continuing education courses.)

New teachers have more incentive to attend university classes as opposed to other kinds of staff development because salaries are connected to the number of college credits earned after a bachelor's degree. Teachers can receive raises for every fifteen to thirty credits they earn. (The number of credits required for a raise is different for each school district.) Also, courses can help certified teachers earn endorsements for specific areas of instruction such as biology or special education.

What Are Endorsements?

Endorsements indicate that teachers have spent a certain amount of time studying a particular topic, and teachers are required to be endorsed for the subjects and grade levels they teach. For example, elementary K–8 certification allows you to teach any subject for children in kindergarten through eighth grade. A subject-specific endorsement is necessary for teaching high school courses and certain subjects that all grades take such as physical education or music.

Which continuing education university courses are offered—or required—are reflections of federal and state mandates (e.g., disaster preparedness or the safe handling of hazardous materials), district emphasis (e.g., reading instruction or technology), and community and school culture (e.g., diversity, discipline policy, or working with English language learners). Some universities offer college credit for courses that may or may not help a classroom teacher. I once took a distance-learning kinesiology course that just required me to watch events during the Goodwill Games and do some journaling about what I saw (as part of earning a physical education endorsement). I passed the class but quickly forgot what I had learned.

While universities provide many courses that are beneficial for teachers and their students, the content may or may not be immediately applicable. The credits earned, which in some places must be preapproved by a teacher's school or district, are helpful in increasing teachers' salaries and maintaining or enhancing certification. However, connecting university utopian ideals touted in the coursework to day-to-day operations in public schools is challenging—and another reason why districts offer their own staff development.

District-Led Courses and Events

They Spent How Much?

A 2015 study by the New Teacher Project estimated that the school districts they studied spent nearly $18,000 per teacher each year on professional development. This indicates that the largest fifty school districts in the United States spend at least $8 million annually on professional development.[12]

Universities are not the only places where educators learn. Districts offer continuing education classes that directly support their goals. For example, a district that emphasizes writing and critical thinking might provide a series of classes for elementary teachers about getting students to write effective five-paragraph essays. Districts often employ a "train-the-trainer" model for their courses, so in this case, they might hire a local teacher who is knowledgeable about essay writing to train her colleagues.

While a few are in it for the extra pay or prestige only, similar to some committee volunteers discussed in Chapter 5, most teachers who are hired to train their colleagues are often quite skilled and do it because they are passionate about the topic and care deeply about helping others. One positive aspect of this type of continuing education is the availability for follow-up; a local instructor can answer questions or provide additional training throughout the year, which typically isn't possible when out-of-town experts are hired.

Sometimes districts bring in published university professors to teach staff. While these "experts" can be dynamic, influential speakers, this type of continuing education may be costly. At an elementary school where I worked in 2004, one such expert was paid $4,000 (plus expenses) to give one ninety-minute presentation to teachers and conduct two seminars for principals and teacher leaders. I was told that the funds were from an account that had to be spent on professional development. It seemed a lot of money to spend for a small amount of training.

While it may seem like a good idea to gather a large group together to learn from an expert, it is fairly disruptive to teachers and students and can have hidden costs that exceed the expert's fees. For example, a district where I was working was trying to make some big changes in special education, so they hired a local university professor to lead a daylong, six-hour workshop. All elementary schools in the district sent a team to a local church (the only place able to handle a group of that size). Each team consisted of the principal, a special education teacher, one or two remedial educators (people who work with special education groups and focus primarily on reading and mathematics), a vice principal/head teacher, and maybe a classroom teacher.

Each school then had to provide coverage for the principals attending the workshop—a staff member (most schools have a "principal designee" for times when the principal is out) whose regular duties were sidelined for the day or a substitute teacher was brought in. Special education sessions at the schools were either canceled, or substitutes were brought in. If they were canceled, then most likely the special education students just stayed in their regular classrooms, adrift in activities and lessons they were unfamiliar with and perhaps didn't even understand. If substitutes were hired, they probably dealt with many behavior problems because special education students often struggle with changes in routines. Substitutes also had to cover duties like lunchroom or playground supervision. It's likely the whole day for the students, substitutes, and staff at these schools was chaotic and unproductive.

Yet the workshop went on. The professor spent the first couple of hours presenting lots of data in a PowerPoint. Each table of attendees then discussed what was presented and how to implement the concepts—at least that was the idea. The group at my table spent the first half hour talking about a playground problem from the day before (a discussion led by a principal). We then tried to figure out how to share with the other teachers our take on what was presented, which took us through to lunch. In the afternoon, time was reserved for questions and more work time at each table. About an hour after lunch, a few people (with phones out) left early. The amount of resources used to conduct this daylong workshop seemed disproportionate to the positive impact on students. The only benefit I received was to learn what some administrators thought was "great stuff" and believed would increase test scores for special education students.

It is interesting that continuing education for teachers, like other professionals, is often in the form of lectures or interactive seminars that happen once a year. While being exposed to something once can make a difference, like the time the principal from Texas did a presentation on how she turned around a poorly performing high school, it's difficult to sustain what you've learned when there is no follow-up. In fact, research has shown that for teachers to successfully implement a new strategy or significantly improve their performance, professional development should be ongoing, yet these one-shot workshops are the norm.[13]

Another factor that affects the uptake and application of information in continuing education courses is the quality of the instruction—the most influential factor in student learning for children *and* adults. Unfortunately, it's a consideration that is often overlooked regardless of whether continuing education courses are district-led or otherwise. One year, I was teaching sixth grade at one of three schools that had the highest poverty rates and lowest test scores in my particular district.

These schools joined together for a daylong staff development seminar on a new mathematics program.

An interesting aspect of working with groups of educators—remember these are all people who have college degrees and who mostly excelled in school—is the contradiction between what they expect of children and how they themselves behave in a classroom setting. Similar to other workshops I had attended, a few folks walked in late. Everyone fumbled with coffee, food, phones, and materials for the class. Side conversations went on, sometimes to the point where the facilitator had to remind folks of expectations. It created a creepy, awkward feeling of being a child again with the teacher going off. Nothing like an uncomfortable atmosphere of learning to build enthusiasm for the content. (Although we do this to children all the time!)

"Thank you all for being here today," the publisher's representative began. Her voice was confident. "I'm excited about working with you all and hope you walk away feeling more comfortable about using the mathematics series. Before we get into the math, I have a fun activity for us . . ."

She asked us to name something we had done over the past two months, like reading a silly romance novel. And whoever had done the same thing was supposed to stand up and say, "Just like me!" Then one of the people standing said something else they did, and we went around for about ten minutes until everyone had a chance to offer up a tidbit about themselves. While I understand the point of building trust, maybe having a little fun, and helping the facilitator get to know a little about the audience, it mostly seemed like a big waste of time. (Though it was a way to do something with the folks who were on time and allowed for stragglers to come in late and not miss the serious content.)

Finally, the staff development began. Teachers were grouped by grade level, so there were about eleven teachers in each classroom, and each room had a facilitator, some from the publisher and some who were teachers in the district who had been trained to teach us. I was in a room with the other sixth-grade teachers, and our facilitator was a woman who had about three years' teaching experience.

"It's important to do the activities before you teach them," she said. "That way you can anticipate student difficulties and offer ways to help them."

While her statement may seem obvious, a surprising number of teachers don't always perform tasks before asking their students to do them, which can lead to frustration all around.

"Please start by going over the materials you have at your table groups," the facilitator said.

After going through the materials provided with the textbooks, and the containers used to organize and store them (these containers are not provided, thus an out-of-pocket expense for teachers), the facilitator started to draw a picture on the overhead projector.

"Excuse me, when will we get enough materials for our whole class?" asked one of the teachers. "I have twenty-eight students and materials for twenty."

Lots of heads nodded and a few teachers said things like "I was wondering that also."

"And the program requires us to make hundreds of copies," the teacher continued. "Our machine is broken half the time. What are we supposed to do?"

The facilitator tried to maintain focus on what she was teaching, but she was continually interrupted by some of the workshop participants. One of the more assertive teachers asked with a touch of attitude, "I heard another teacher say the book doesn't prepare the kids for the test. Why are we using it?" As the day wore on, the atmosphere grew more confrontational—and awkward. I kept thinking perhaps the facilitator could acknowledge the teachers' frustrations yet point out she could not change those things, so we could just get on with the lessons. The lack of professionalism—on the part of the facilitator and the teachers in the workshop—made this an unnecessarily painful and ineffective staff development experience.

However, I heard the fourth-grade teachers had a different workshop experience. Their facilitator, a woman with about six years' teaching experience, set the tone immediately. "It's so cool to work with you all today as you make sense of the math program. I know how hard it is, especially when you have so many students with such a range of abilities. Let's start by taking a moment to reflect on what has gone well so far this year." After a few minutes of silent writing, the teachers share:

"The students are given lots of problem-solving activities."

"Yes, and they're not only using new skills, but reviewing old ones too."

"The hands-on materials are so good for my kinesthetic students."

After a few minutes of sharing the good, the facilitator said, "Now, please write down any questions or concerns you have about the program. Please understand I cannot buy you more time in the day—there is never enough time for a teacher. I also cannot fix the copy machine, take away the state test, or lessen your countless other duties. However, we can share ideas on what's working practically in classrooms." There were lots of nodding heads and murmurs of "Good, maybe we can get to the real stuff" and "Works for me." Their day was full of productive work and even some laughter.

Though each group went through two units of the program, following established lesson plans as best they could, the quality of the day varied greatly. Some groups of teachers came away angry, feeling they had wasted their time. Some were frustrated with the facilitators. I heard comments like "Can you believe she is the one teaching us? She's only been teaching for three years, and I've been here twenty-two."

"I was going crazy every time she clapped her hands to get our attention. I'm not in first grade!"

Other frustrations were about the program itself. "There is too much reading involved. My kids just don't get it."

"The teacher's manual doesn't make sense even now. He kept saying flip back to this tab or that tab. I got lost. I'm just going to do my own thing. I don't care."

There were also positive comments. "I really liked how we got to actually do the activities like the kids will. That helps."

"I have lots of ideas about how I'm going to manage math time now. Very practical day."

"Wasn't our facilitator good? She had such practical knowledge and a great sense of humor!"

As discussed in Chapter 3, it is the individual teacher who makes a huge difference in the effectiveness of a learning experience—no matter how old the students are. How teachers are supported, what coursework is provided, and who teaches those courses all influence their practice and thus, students as well.

School-Led Staff Development

Individual schools have their own professional development that (hopefully) applies directly to the needs of their students and staff. For example, some schools use unique discipline policies or have specific methods of teaching reading or mathematics that are effective for their student population—thus a need for custom continuing education coursework. It also plays into many teachers' attitudes that what they deal with is exceptional and that they need different support than other places, which may or may not be true.

The structure of school-led professional development is often flexible, allowing for multiple one- to two-hour sessions rather than whole-day workshops, which are easier to schedule. Another advantage of school-led staff development is that follow-up training is possible at regular intervals, during weekly or monthly staff meetings. School leadership determines what the content of the classes will be. (Whatever administration supports and emphasizes will tend to show up in these classes, and thus student lessons—especially if it's included in evaluations.) Typically, principals will teach the classes with another building or district-level leader to facilitate. Sometimes even a person from outside the district will be hired to help, depending on the cost.

An advantage of having someone within the building conduct the sessions is their prior knowledge about the staff—not just which room works best for everyone, who will need to process out loud, or what snacks are most popular, but what their specific needs are in regard to classroom support, so the workshop can be tailored to address those needs. For example, in a school focusing on improving reading skills in all subjects, leadership conducts a presentation on questioning strategies. Afterward, the teachers break out into grade-level teams and work on the particular subject area where reading comprehension is a challenge. The third-grade team might focus on their current science unit, while the fifth-grade team focuses on upcoming social studies projects.

There are a few disadvantages to school-based professional development. The small number of teacher participants limits the amount of diverse ideas and experiences shared. Also, interpersonal issues among staff can sometimes get in the way of learning; for example, if the presenter is not someone well-liked or if there are groups of teachers who just do not work well together. Whether professional development is run by districts or schools, there will be pluses and minuses. Thus, leadership's careful planning for a variety of structures, including personalized support, is so important.

Within buildings and grade levels, individual teachers can have different strengths and areas that need improving. Group professional development won't necessarily address those areas, but one-on-one support can.

Coaching

A common professional development practice that is helpful in enhancing any skill is coaching. This is a growing aspect of staff development in education; there are conferences and lots of literature devoted to the practice and implementation of coaching. One of the benefits of coaching is that it can encourage teachers to try new techniques or resources. In fact, studies have shown that coaching is one of the most effective ways to help teachers master a new skill or simply improve their practice.[14] It's easier for them to implement new practices if they have consistent, supportive feedback. Individual support can address a person's unique situation and needs versus group trainings, where the content may or may not apply. Coaching is also a valuable tool for teachers who are reserved and may have trouble speaking up in large groups. Perhaps the biggest advantage is that coaches visit classrooms and see the action; firsthand observation through fresh eyes can be helpful.

There are three key elements of successful coaching. The first is teacher motivation—in order for coaching to be effective, teachers must want to grow and improve their craft. This means taking a clear-eyed look at what they do well and what needs improvement, without getting defensive so that, ideally, they can take the lead in establishing goals.

Another important aspect of coaching is trust. A coach should not be an administrator or anyone who holds evaluative power over the teacher. A coach's sole purpose should be to support teachers by honoring their strengths, listening carefully, asking clarifying questions, helping identify reasonable goals, providing nonjudgmental feedback, and facilitating honest self-reflection.

Administration plays a big role in fostering trust between coaches and teachers. For example, they must support the relationship without managing it, respecting the confidential nature of the coach-teacher relationship and acknowledging a teacher's commitment to improving their practice. Leadership should also be patient and not expect immediate perfection. One factor that can impede trust is when coaches are imposed on teachers, poor student test scores being a major reason. It can create a strained relationship between coach and teacher from the start, making for interactions that aren't necessarily open or productive.

The third important aspect of coaching is honoring the time commitment involved. It can be difficult to find the time for goal setting, observations, and post-observation review, which are all important parts of the coaching process. Some principals will pay for substitutes to cover for teachers so they can meet with coaches; others simply hope it happens before or after school, on top of all the other duties teachers must fulfill.

Time can also be an issue for coaches too, particularly if they are primarily supporting one subject, often reading or mathematics. In many elementary schools, reading and mathematics instruction occurs at set times during the day. If every class is teaching reading at the same time, a coach can only be in one place at that time. If a school has two or three teachers for each grade level, then one coach can only be in each teacher's class maybe once every few weeks, making consistent support difficult.

As helpful as this staff development tool can be, sometimes it's not in the budget to hire professional educational coaches. In the midnineties, a rough form of "peer coaching" was brought to one school where I was teaching sixth grade. Each teacher was paired with another teacher from the same building. As a peer, our only job was to support a colleague by setting a measurable goal, like tracking where in class a teacher stood or counting the number of times a teacher called on girls versus boys. Judgments and opinions about the way lessons were taught was not part of the deal. I did not find the process useful, partly because it seemed contrived and partly because there was no follow-up. However, the structure of peer coaching has improved since then, making this form of professional development more of a worthwhile endeavor.

Despite my not-so-helpful peer coaching experience, I was inspired by the concept, and ended up becoming a coach toward the end of my career. My main area of focus was mathematics in elementary schools, though I worked in other content areas as well. As a coach, I hoped to have a positive impact, indirectly, on more students than I could reach in my classroom, and I considered myself an advocate for both students and teachers. But regardless of my idealism, serving as a coach was not always an easy role. Some of my experiences were positive . . . and some were not.

When I started coaching, it was in a new district, and not having prior relationships with the teachers I was supporting added to the challenge. Because I was assigned to certain buildings—those with some of the lowest test scores in the district—I was greeted with mixed feelings. Teachers did not request me; administration told me which schools and which grade levels to work with. At first, most teachers thought of me as just another suit from the central office (albeit one who wore Tigger ties) that was there to criticize them. I understood the skepticism—after all, I had been in their shoes. But once people got to know me and witnessed me working with students, I was able to establish trust with many teachers. In fact, some teachers even sought me out for support about instructional practices. Unfortunately, there were also those who just didn't want to see me at all, no matter what.

Some teachers, especially ones with many years of experience, can be resistant to anyone helping because they view it as a threat. They may feel that succumbing to coaching means they are a bad teacher and have been doing things wrong for years when they thought they were successful. Also, many teachers are skeptical of anything administration supports.

The teachers who were open to support were easiest to work with—our discussions were focused on the teaching and learning of mathematics; we had regular meetings, and more often than not, student achievement increased. Though it was ultimately the students who showed improvement, I felt I was a part of the success. Schools I supported had measurable increases (between 5 percent and 32 percent) in students meeting standard on mathematics tests. However, what was most rewarding to me was when I was able to help students and teachers actually enjoy mathematics.

In addition to coaching teachers, another part of my duties was to model mathematics lessons using district-approved resources. There is some value in seeing a different way of teaching a skill like finding the area of a triangle. However, a coach and a teacher may have different ways of interacting with students, thus modeling of lessons is only so effective.

Teaching is partly performance art. Like skilled actors and athletes, teachers can benefit from coaching a lot. (Remember the skills discussed in Chapter 3—like how to keep a group of children focused, disciplined, and behaving respectfully, and what instructional methods work for auditory, kinesthetic, and visual learners?) Coaching models lifelong learning for students and colleagues, especially when the most respected teachers are willing to learn and grow in their practice. Coaching is even more beneficial to teaching and learning as teachers progress in their careers and technology evolves—and also because children and their needs do change over time.

Learning with Peers

It's common for teachers to feel a sense of isolation—the responsibilities of the job can weigh heavily, and without regular adult interaction to share the burden, the stress can lead to burnout. Many administrators try to combat this sense of isolation by establishing professional learning communities at their schools, where teachers collaborate frequently with each other (and administration). This is another form of staff development—when small groups of teachers work together.

Peer learning can be informal; for example, when two or more teachers are working on a similar goal, like reading fiction and nonfiction books that complement the social studies text. They provide support and encouragement for each other by checking in now and then to see how each is progressing, or they may meet weekly to review reading lists and lesson plans.

Peer learning can also take a more formal, structured approach, particularly during new textbook adoptions. Teachers of the same grade levels in elementary schools (or subjects in middle and high schools) will get together and plan lessons for the week or month (or however long a particular unit of study lasts). Those meeting times are usually set by principals at the beginning of the year. The goal is not only to have a collaborative working environment but also to anticipate and minimize challenges associated with teaching the new content.

Throughout my career, I have learned a lot from peer interactions; however, sometimes personality conflicts interfere with group work. Hence, the effectiveness of peer learning as a form of professional development is highly dependent on the makeup of the peer group. One year during the fall, I was teaching sixth grade at a school that had just adopted a new mathematics program. The other sixth-grade teachers and I were meeting to discuss lesson planning and report cards. While it could and should have been a useful opportunity to bounce ideas off each other, it fell far short.

It was a wet gray afternoon, which is often the case in October in Seattle. You'd think people would get used to the gloom, but this time of year grumpiness abounds and griping becomes more common, about everything—the weather, students, parents, administration, curriculum, and upcoming report cards.

"I'm spending so much time on math and reading. I haven't taught any science, barely touched on social studies, let alone the Halloween art lessons that kids used to enjoy so much," asserted Ms. Killjoy, the most experienced teacher (twenty years) in the group. "There just isn't enough time to prepare and teach anything else."

The first time you work with a new program, it takes more prep time. The pacing of lessons doesn't always go as smoothly as it does when teachers use the resources they're used to. Mathematics programs, for several reasons, seem to be particularly difficult in this respect. Part of it is math phobia. Part of it is how programs are purchased and implemented (all grades at once), which means many of the students don't have the knowledge base necessary to succeed. Therefore, teachers must take extra time to help them develop it. And of course, teachers are human beings, not robots, so they need time to become adept with new resources, which they may or may not like or see the value of. Part of it is also that many mathematics programs are structured differently than the way they used to be, the way many teachers are familiar with. Thus the necessity for peer support and collaboration among teachers. While I empathized with Ms. Killjoy to an extent, we weren't there to complain. I was the second most experienced teacher in the group with seven years on the job, and by then it was plain to me that never having enough time just goes with the territory. What's the point of dwelling on it?

I tried to nudge the meeting along. "We're supposed to talk about the new math program and see if maybe we can help each other. We should also talk about how we're going to fill out report cards. The quarter's ending soon, and conferences aren't far off."

My effort to get to the point was ignored. The group just continued chatting. "I like it, but I never know where to find the answers," said Ms. Sullivan with a frown. She was the youngest, least experienced teacher among us.

"You're supposed to be able to do the math yourself . . . but the answers are in the teacher resource manual." I think, I *hope*, I said this with a smile. I wasn't trying to be rude exactly, but come on—if you can't come up with the answer on your own, then you've got bigger problems than not being able to find the right page for the solutions. Sadly, my attitude was not positive.

Ignoring my comment, Ms. Sullivan said, "We spent all that time in August on this stuff, and it seems a lot different when the students are there. I hear some schools are having study groups of teachers every week. They say it's helping."

"That's why we are here now, to see how we can support each other with the new texts," Ms. Killjoy said with a tinge of snark. "I still don't see why we had to adopt this text. I liked the old texts, and my students all got good grades."

And on and on it went. This is a meeting where a coach could have helped by setting a positive tone, possibly by pointing out how great it is to have time scheduled for collaboration. We were not a tight-knit group, which is not uncommon. Our grade-level meetings were not the most productive or friendly. Just because we taught the same grade at the same school, did not mean we automatically liked each other—also, not uncommon. Having a coach to facilitate the meeting would have helped to keep us on task. (Adults are not always self-disciplined.)

Contrast the meeting described above with one several years later when I was working as a coach. Again the meeting was about mathematics, but this time with a focus on upcoming lessons about measurement.

I was with Ms. Johannson and Ms. Caldwell in Ms. Caldwell's room, where she had taught fifth grade for the past twelve years. We were waiting for another fifth-grade teacher to show up. I had been going to that school two days a week for the past several months to support teachers in their mathematics instruction. The fifth-grade "team" didn't like each other and struggled to get along, a fact one of them shared with me often. The school had a lot of student turnover. Many students were reading below grade level, and about 75 percent of them received free or reduced-price lunches. Discipline was a constant issue—it was not an easy place to teach.

"I hope we get out of here quickly," Ms. Johannson said. "I've got to get my daughter from cheer practice."

"We have to wait for Janice," stated Ms. Caldwell sharply as she gathered some papers at her desk. "And we *all* would rather not be here." She glared at me.

You'd have to be dead or unconscious not to feel the tension in the room. I made a feeble attempt to dispel the bad vibes, asking the group about their plans for the long weekend. I got a few terse responses and then, thankfully, Ms. Bonner (Janice), a good friend of Ms. Caldwell's, swept in. "I'm sorry—I was on the phone with Jason's mother," she said.

"That family has had issues for years. How did it go?" Ms. Caldwell asked. Before that question could be answered, I jumped in. "With time being precious, could we get to the math and save that for later?"

"Remember, I have to pick up my daughter, so let's get started," Ms. Johannson said.

Ms. Caldwell rolled her eyes.

Luckily, Ms. Bonner said, "I need to not think about it now anyway. Let's get into the math."

We then started to review upcoming lessons from the text, talking about how to get the students to measure objects and how to document their findings. The interaction was cordial, but with an edge. I knew they didn't want to be there.

"The main goal of these lessons is to get students familiar with estimating and finding lengths, weights, and volumes, but you can have some fun with it, maybe hold a Measurement Olympics. I got this activity years ago in a workshop." I explained about how to set up the "events" (stations), for example, a weight-lifting event where they measured how much a handful of marbles weighed or a throwing event where they measured how far they could toss a paper straw "javelin."

Ms. Caldwell (who had been fairly negative about math ever since I had first come to the school) sat up straight and got a little wide-eyed. "I thought we had to only use the text," she said, hopping up and getting a plastic storage tub from a stack in the corner. "I have all the score sheets for this already. We did this several years ago before all the stupid testing. The kids loved it and it really helps. Are you sure it's OK to do this?"

I explained to her and the others that as long as they were teaching the skills articulated in the standards, using other materials to supplement the main text, especially hands-on resources, is perfectly OK and even encouraged when appropriate. As she got the items out of the tub, I asked her if she would demonstrate how to do the activities. The mood in the room became much lighter (even with rain falling outside) as we went through some of the "events." The meeting ended on time with Ms. Caldwell, Ms. Bonner, and Ms. Johannson excitedly brainstorming about prizes and how to chart the results of all classes for comparison.

Having an outside facilitator helped buffer some ill will between the teachers so that the focus could be handled professionally. I was lucky to hit on something that Ms. Caldwell liked, and we were able to accomplish the main goal of having the teachers review what they were about to teach and know what standards to address in those lessons. It didn't hurt that they knew I had over fifteen years of successful teaching experience in schools similar to theirs. We avoided unnecessary conflict because none of the three had to be in charge of the others. And my only role was to support their teaching. Since I was not part of their personal or professional issues—nor would I allow myself to become mixed up in them—we were able to keep the peer meeting on task and productive.

Peers can be influential. Once trust and respect are established, the results can be positive. Having a person who is only there to support teachers and help them hone their teaching ability—with optimizing student learning as the main goal—is a great part of what happens in education.

Who Should Take the Lead?

Ultimately, teachers themselves are responsible for self-monitoring their learning and professionalism, but there is room for improvement in providing consistent, meaningful learning opportunities for teachers to hone their craft. For example, scheduling workshops at 4:00 or 4:30 p.m.—after a full day of teaching—is not ideal for stamina, motivation, or retention of the material, especially when dogs need to be walked and hunger prevails. Yet often teachers and administrators must attend those late-afternoon classes for two to three hours, trying to be attentive. Course content should focus on strategies for improvement, rather than dwelling on what teachers are doing wrong. Consistent follow-up training during the implementation period for these strategies is vital; otherwise, improvement is unlikely to continue. Required staff development coursework should be periodically evaluated for relevancy and usefulness. For example, demanding teachers learn a computer program when there are only two computers per classroom for twenty-eight children is likely a waste of time and resources. It's important to bear in mind what motivates teachers and what doesn't. Simply improving test scores is not likely to garner much buy-in, but appealing to their passion for furthering the profession and for improving student engagement may spark their interest. It's also helpful to celebrate successes, because there is no shortage of people noting the failures and how to correct them.

"The teachers need to . . ." (fill in the blank with whatever) is a statement many administrators, parents, politicians, and even some teachers make—predominately as a reaction to low test scores, a school incident, or some practice that supposedly worked somewhere else and was presented or written up in a magazine. Particularly in elementary schools, teachers are required to teach—and thus spend countless hours learning about—all sorts of things that go beyond reading and math, such as conflict resolution, social skills, drug education, sex education, the integration of special education students, and how to work with students of poverty. Some of it is very useful, yet when the emphasis changes, which it often does, good lessons learned and practiced can be pushed aside. Consistency is lost.

This is part of why the teachers union should be leading professional development—hopefully bringing more vision and less reaction to what supports teachers the best so they can provide quality educational experiences for all children. Coaching is one area where unions could take the lead. Of course, administration and the community should all have input. A healthy collaborative leadership model that keeps students' success as the prime directive would make a huge difference in keeping staff development relevant and productive. Ongoing support of teachers is a key part of improving public education. Even the best and brightest teachers can benefit from support about their choices in the classroom.

Again, if we had a clear purpose for public schools, and leadership worked with staff, teachers unions, and communities in keeping those goals (children's futures) at the forefront, then all professional development would follow those goals. Without support of teachers and staff through ongoing coursework, the greatest of ideas can fall by the wayside. Schools and communities both have a role to play in establishing cultures that support teachers in their quest for lifelong learning.

Chapter 7

School Culture: What Shapes a Learning Environment?

What's the Vibe?

Anytime you gather a few hundred people in one place on a daily basis, it will have a particular culture, a unique atmosphere and way of doing things. Schools are no exception. School culture includes the prevailing behaviors and attitudes of the people in the school, young and old—how the school functions and how it feels to be there. What is emphasized? What is valued? How do people interact? These basic aspects of school culture will manifest in different ways.

For example, a school can be a warm, friendly place of learning or a cold, rule-dominated building filled with conflict. Humans have a basic need for safety; if children do not feel safe, then they will have a hard time concentrating on lessons. Negative emotions such as frustration, anger, or fear distract from positive interactions and learning. Similar to what teachers choose to emphasize in their classrooms, what a school as a whole emphasizes will trigger emotional reactions, from reassurance and joy to resentment and anxiety. The culture of a school can foster a positive learning environment—or not.

Examples and Elements of School Culture

There are many factors that shape a school's culture, but before we explore the individual aspects, let's take a look at where I worked to demonstrate just how different the cultures of two schools, both in the same district, can be.

Apple Tree Elementary School, for grades kindergarten through six, was composed of many students who lived in low-income apartments, single-family homes that were lower-middle class, and a lot of duplex and fourplex rentals. After dark, it was not a safe area to walk around. About 75 percent of the students received free or reduced lunch prices and over forty languages were spoken in students' homes. About 40 percent of the students were white. The school had an English Language Learner program for children brand-new to the country. There was quite a bit of turnover among the students, with families moving in and out of the area each month, but about one-third of the more than five hundred students stayed all seven years.

Most of the staff were white, female (only two nonwhite teachers and only a couple of male teachers), and experienced—there were only a few newer teachers. There was little turnover among staff. The teachers strove to reach all learners, honored and liked the diversity, but also struggled with relating to some parents. Reading and mathematics were celebrated, and students achieved above-average success for their demographics. Behavior was a constant issue with some staff, and there was a certain amount of inconsistency in what was tolerated. In other words, some teachers had short fuses and others not so much. Yet it was safe. The office staff was dedicated, efficient, and welcoming. About six families ran all the PTA functions and provided valued support.

Teaching and learning were the obvious priorities—and celebrated at Apple Tree. It was a comfortable place for young and old. While frequent intervention was necessary to keep behaviors from getting out of control, the school functioned fairly smoothly most days. Even the children who often exhibited behavior problems on the playground or in classes liked going to that school. The adults, staff, and parents (with a few exceptions) all supported the children and their learning. The leadership strove to create a positive learning community, which is part of why staff turnover was low.

Like Apple Tree Elementary, Fir Tree Elementary School was only about fifteen miles from downtown Seattle, but it had a different culture. Students who attended Fir Tree lived in a mix of low-income apartments, though mostly single-family homes and other rentals. About half of the students lived on safe streets and could play outside; the other half lived near a major thoroughfare with some unsavory activity. About 40 percent of the children received free or reduced lunch prices, almost double the percentage just ten years earlier. About 75 percent of the students were white, and only a few students did not speak English at home.

The principal was a fairly weak leader, and the staff did what they wanted. Rules were inconsistent, and the children's behavior was an issue for a few teachers. About half the grades had teachers who liked each other, collaborated often, and had been there for a while, eight to twenty-five years. The other teachers just kept to themselves, rarely collaborated, and almost never went in the staff room for lunch. The office staff, while cordial to most school personnel, was gruff and terse with parents and children. There were three paraprofessionals who were assertive and either liked you or made it clear they would like to see you hung from the rafters. Along with a couple of the more experienced teachers, they would dominate discussion in the staff room, where a lot of wishing for things from the past happened: "Why can't we sing Christmas carols?" "Those kids aren't like they used to be—look at what they wear to school." Some staff worked hard to reach all students, and some seemed to blame the students for not learning. The whole staff was white. The school had about ten families that ran the PTA and provided support for classroom teachers. The students, who had been at the school since kindergarten, mostly did well academically, but the others struggled a lot.

Fir Tree had a disjointed culture with no direction. Adults and children each had their cliques, creating distinct areas of the school that seemed independent of one another. The newer students struggled to fit in, though many tight friendships were formed and evident on the playground. An edgy feeling permeated the building. The adults were often temperamental and did not put energy into creating a positive learning community. Rather, they seemed more interested in their own little worlds and the way things used to be.

Those two schools were in the same region and had similar demographics but very different cultures. Why? The most significant reason was the difference in the way the principals and teachers interacted with each other, as well as the students and parents. The collaboration of the staff, the welcoming atmosphere, and concerted effort to teach all students at Apple Tree, contrasted with the disjointed efforts and disgruntled personnel at Fir Tree. While both schools experienced success with students who attended long term, the staff had different expectations for diverse learners, which was reflected in student behavior both socially and academically.

When seeking to improve student achievement, a school's culture needs to be acknowledged. Each school is composed of unique individuals that contribute to its culture, so trying to replicate what was successful at another school, highly touted or not, is not likely to produce the desired results. Each building, like each student, should be treated individually, capitalizing on strengths and bolstering weaknesses.

Any organization that has people with positive attitudes working hard toward a common goal will, in general, have more success and sustainability than a place with discontented staff members who are each in pursuit of their own agenda. Schools are no exception. Students will mostly adapt to the culture of whatever school they attend. A positive environment focused on learning will have happier and more successful students overall than a place where conflicts are frequent and negative attitudes prevail. While attitudes are a significant aspect of school culture, they're not the only factor. The deeper you look into what influences school culture, the more complicated it gets. As you will see, the onion has many layers to it.

School Size

The size of a school matters. A small school with only twenty staff members and three hundred students will have a different feel with different needs than a school with seventy-five staff members and eight hundred students.

One K–6 school where I worked was a center for severely challenged students with disorders such as down syndrome and cerebral palsy.

With only eight regular education classroom teachers and just over two hundred students, it was different than a K–6 school with over six hundred students and three or four teachers for each grade level. There were eight special needs classrooms, with six to ten students each, that had a certified teacher and maybe two or three other specially trained adults. Staff meetings (another part of school culture) would get interesting sometimes as the number of special education teachers was about three times that of regular education teachers, since they had different interests.

The students who did not move away spent up to seven years (K–6) with the same classmates, which had its pluses and minuses—strong friendships and strong dislikes. Some cohorts were more trouble than others because of lingering issues between students (or families). But a significant aspect of the school's culture was focused on including the special needs children as much as possible. There was a lot of acceptance of differences and seeing past physical limitations, evident during recess, where students in wheelchairs were included in games like tetherball or four square. Those relationships and interactions were part of that school's unique culture.

Organization of Grade Levels

What is the best way to group grade levels in a school? There are many models with varying degrees of success and reasons for the configurations. Most elementary schools comprise kindergarten through fifth or sixth grade. Yet some places have grades K–3 and 4–6, or K–2 and 3–5, or K–8. Most middle schools comprise grades 6–8, 7–8, or 7–9, though I've heard of 5–7. Most high schools contain grades 9–12 or 10–12. There are many places that have K–12 programs as well.

Why all the variety? What is the ideal configuration for all children? *Is* there one ideal grade configuration for schools? Part of the variation is due to a community's population, also budgets and school board decisions.

Middle school students, in particular, can be perplexing for adults to both teach and organize into appropriate grade levels. Adults tend to have a hard time working with children who are entering puberty and are hormonally unbalanced. I can attest to the high energy and severe mood swings, the "life-threatening" drama that can unfold at any moment. They are, in general, babies in big bodies who want to be adults, make decisions for themselves, and have romantic relationships while at the same time remain irresponsible and taken care of ("Mom, have you seen my shoes?").

When one district changed configurations, going from a 7–9 junior high school and a 10–12 high school to a 7–8 middle school and 9–12 high school, it was interesting to see the differences in how the same group of students was viewed. The ninth graders at the junior high school had been the mature, helpful leaders and were mourned by many teachers when they left. This same group of "leaders" then became the immature "can't find their head on their shoulders" pains-in-the-rear that high school teachers dreaded having to teach. Same children, different outlook.

It is challenging for many adults to remember how difficult adolescence was or to understand how hard it is now. Not many people look back at those middle years with fondness. Also, it's easy to forget how much difference one, two, three, or four years can make in a young person's life, especially when you are not the top dog or in with the "cool" people. I remember being intimidated, awed by, and scared of the people two to four years ahead of me in school, especially in junior high and as a high school freshman.

The age range of the students in a school influences how the school functions and shapes the kinds of interactions had in hallways, playgrounds, and lunchrooms. (For example, a miserable lunch encounter—being bullied by an older peer or having no one to sit with—can ruin one's day. On the other hand, a timely smile from a fellow student and shared laughter can make one's day the best ever.) The configuration of grade levels in schools is too complex an issue for one solution. It is up to localities to do what is best for children while also maintaining a high standard of quality. Yet it is another facet of public education that should be considered when approaching reform.

Individual Class Configurations

The way students are grouped at the classroom level can affect how that classroom functions and, ultimately, how the school functions. Each group of students brings a unique set of challenges. Often it only takes one strong personality (a bully, a clown, a constant talker, or one who insists on being first to answer) to change the whole dynamic of a classroom. With the goal of minimizing challenges for teachers and providing an appropriate learning environment for each student, all kinds of placement methods are used in schools. Some use test data, for example, while others look at individual students to see who might work best with a particular teacher, or whatever criteria the school deems best. In reality, though, a lot of smart students are stuck in classes that don't challenge them, and from early on they are not given a chance to engage or shine. A school's culture is not only affected by how students are selected but also how teachers react to their class lists.

One of the first things many teachers do when they get their class list is to count how many special education and Title I children they have. (Title I is a label assigned to children who are in need of extra help but do not qualify for special education.) Many teachers assess the gender balance—or lack thereof among the students—and make judgments before seeing how the students actually get along. ("Oh man, eighteen boys and only nine girls is going to be a mess.") Looking for certain names of students is also common—those with reputations or notorious siblings. Some teachers will comb through students' cumulative files carefully and talk with their students' previous teachers to get an idea of what to expect. So without meeting the children, teachers often judge and categorize them, and a teacher's bias will influence how they interact with students—a central part of school culture.

I felt it was important to wait to meet each student in person before drawing any conclusions about their abilities and temperaments. I listened to them, looked at the work they produced, and then I would determine if extra help or other adaptations were called for. Giving students a clean slate to start each year is important. One reason being that significant growth happens during the summer break. Think about it this way, ten weeks to a ten-year-old is proportionate to thirty weeks for a thirty-year-old. Much can happen in that time—old habits can fall by the wayside as attitudes and perspectives mature. Each year, I was intentional about beginning the journey with my students in a fresh way, avoiding negative prejudgments.

Most school staff will say that they are doing their best not to prejudge students by race or wealth, but by actual achievement. However, looking at placement statistics often shows otherwise. In general, special education is disproportionately populated by male students of color, while higher-level gifted programs tend to be populated by whites and Asians.[15] Many people look at a quiet student of Japanese descent and assume he or she is smart. Conversely, a loud Black student will be looked at as trouble, no matter how smart. Often teachers of a quiet white student who is well-dressed though struggling mightily with turning in schoolwork will say, "I know she is capable of better work. Maybe she can come in for some extra help at recess?" Meanwhile, the chatty student of Hispanic heritage who is wearing clean but obviously hand-me-down clothing might actually do a little better than the white student but also struggle to turn in work. Yet the same teacher says, "We need to test Juanita for ADHD and special education. She's never focused and is a disruption."

This is part of why I told students, all my students, that I had to have tangible proof—usually some written assignment or test—to show someone else how smart they were. I couldn't just say, "I know you can do this. Here's your A."

The question of ability brings up another aspect of how to group students: What range of student abilities and skills in one classroom is ideal for children? Heterogeneous classrooms with a healthy mix of student achievement levels can be productive for children. They learn from each other, and each child has different strengths. Homogeneous classrooms are most beneficial to students at both extremes of cognitive abilities. (The students who think differently than the vast majority of people, whether the students are struggling to understand simple sentences or are Mensa material, need different challenges and learning activities.) The mix of students, whether heterogeneous or not, affects how a classroom functions and how children perceive themselves—as smart, capable, gifted, or dumb.

Another aspect of class configurations to consider is the grouping of children according to age. The cognitive and developmental differences between children in the same age group starts in kindergarten. Some five-year-olds are still struggling with toileting issues or unexplained meltdowns, while others are already writing their names, washing their hands without being told, and reading books by Dr. Seuss. Put twenty-five five-year-olds together and you'll have a huge range of abilities from the start, and the gap widens as the children age. It is not unusual for a fifth-grade class of ten-year-olds to have a wide range of abilities, some performing at a second-grade level while others perform at a high school level. For example, one child can solve problems with algebraic equations while another struggles with addition. Despite knowing that children progress and learn at different rates, every child within a particular age group is held to the same standard—the challenge for teachers is huge. While some variety within a classroom is actually good for students, because they learn so much from each other, having such a huge gap in abilities is not ideal.

Students' range of abilities has a significant effect on the daily goings-on in classrooms—how smoothly lessons go and how much teaching and learning (as opposed to misbehavior management, boredom, and confusion) actually take place. As mentioned in Chapter 3, quality teaching takes a student from where they are and helps them learn and grow from that point. There is much information on how teachers can adapt lessons to be accessible to all students (referred to as differentiated instruction). However, it is more practical for classrooms where learning abilities are not so wide-ranging.

To address this issue, elementary schools often try to limit the range of abilities in classrooms by having special programs for students at the extremes of the spectrum. The high-achieving students are separated— the ones who usually have the strongest (or loudest) parental support— and put in "gifted" classes, though many of the students just work hard. Then, the lowest-achieving students are given small group remediation with tutors or special education teachers. They may come and go from their regular classroom so frequently for additional support that they often end up spending a lot of time walking around. Their tutors may not be the most qualified, depending on whom a school can afford to hire. Meanwhile, the middle majority just keeps floating through, maybe to be inspired. Strict adherence to traditional age grouping helps create this problem.

For some children, the challenge to keep up is so daunting that they quickly turn away from school, and more kids do so as the years progress. It is disheartening when they know, and children do know, that they are not understanding what everyone else is getting. Some schools will have children repeat a grade to help them catch up, yet that has all sorts of negative ramifications. A child's behavior in and out of the classroom is influenced by how they feel about their learning. A positive or negative attitude among students will affect how they behave and thus the culture of a school.

To help all students succeed, we must examine how class configurations—and how teachers manage those configurations—support or detract from learning. Accepting that even one child does not receive equitable support and educational opportunities is wrong.

Extracurricular Activities

Extracurricular activities can shape the identity and culture of a school, and in turn have an impact on student achievement. For example, some schools have reputations for strong music, technology, or science programs, or clubs that celebrate cultural or ethnic heritage. Other schools may excel at math competitions, mock trials, chess tournaments, or acrobatics. Still others may have strong advanced placement courses or similar extensions of classroom work. These "extras" can help children thrive by reducing stress, improving time management skills, exposing them to diverse social groups, and helping them find their niche. In my experience, children who have a sense of pride about their school, who are involved in school activities outside the purview of their regular classroom, tend to experience more academic success.

Allowing schools to have different identities based on their offerings is part of what makes school improvement sustainable; they have the latitude to meet the needs of their particular student population. Extracurricular activities are vital to building a sense of community within a school, which in turn fosters academic achievement and personal growth. It's important to remember this aspect of school culture, because when purse strings tighten, money for extracurriculars is often the first to go, which can cut the heart and soul out of a school. Taking away what motivates students and builds a vibrant learning community does not make sense. Conversely, when activities outside the classroom become more important than learning in classrooms— what often happens with sports—it becomes a hindrance to student achievement. A healthy balance is necessary.

School Personnel

While a classroom teacher has the most impact on student success, what the bus driver says or does can make or break a day as well. Paraprofessionals and other noncertified school personnel have a tremendous amount of influence on school culture. Paraprofessionals have various responsibilities in schools, such as tutoring and supporting overloaded classrooms.

Details about Paraprofessionals

Paraprofessionals who work in schools with a Title I program (or similar) must meet minimum language and math requirements.[16] Pay ranges between ten to twenty dollars per hour depending on experience, and they work anywhere from three to thirty hours a week.

Some paraprofessionals monitor recess, which can be a challenging job; typically, only two or three adults are responsible for keeping an eye on a few hundred children. With the best of intentions, like safety first and foremost, many paraprofessionals are controlling. They often engage in power struggles with children, some of whom are legitimately naughty. But many of these conflicts are unnecessary because the children need to run around and shout. The playground is quite a world to itself . . . and very telling about a school's culture.

After recess, incidents from the playground often spill over into the classroom. I had more than one student return from recess upset over what a paraprofessional or teacher on duty had done. My students would say things like "She didn't listen!" or "She doesn't understand soccer!" or "We didn't do anything wrong!" Sadly, many conflicts escalated when paraprofessionals got involved. Sometimes it took a while for the students to focus on learning again, though I made it clear that playground issues were not going to take away from class time and would be dealt with later if necessary. (Unfortunately, it was the adult who sometimes wouldn't let something go.) In some schools, conflicts are so prevalent that social skills and conflict resolution are required for teaching in classrooms, which is revealing about the culture.

Perhaps the most influential paraprofessionals are the classroom aides or tutors. Many places will identify a group of four children in a class or grade level who "need extra help" with math or reading but do not qualify for special education. So they get sent to work with a paraprofessional for fifteen to thirty minutes at a time. How often these aides/tutors meet with students can vary, depending on the school's population.

There were many good paraprofessionals I saw in action (and a few that were not). For example, Ms. Morgan worked mostly with first and second graders. Able to reach even the most squirrely, she knew how far to push each student academically, and her calm, caring demeanor helped children focus on the task in front of them; they would tune into her soft-spoken voice. She was not only an effective reading and mathematics instructor but also gave each child unconditional affection, and for some that was the most positive attention they got all day. Often she would have a thank-you note from a child pinned to her blouse.

The relationships between paraprofessionals and students can be positive; as in the example with Ms. Morgan, their interaction may be the only time a student feels heard and seen. Conversely, if there is a constant power struggle or just a disconnect between the student and paraprofessional, the time is wasted and students are left feeling frustrated. Unfortunately, some of the neediest children are sent to the least-qualified adults. Seems backward. Remember the high school principal who matched the best teachers with the most struggling students and how that turned around student achievement? The idea makes sense, yet it isn't the normal practice.

Like paraprofessionals, office staff are a key aspect of school culture. They serve as the first impression of a school; sadly, many are crabby on a good day. Over the years, I dealt with several office staff members who just didn't like children . . . or parents. On the other hand, some were the sweetest, most welcoming people you could imagine and were a joy to be around.

One day I was in the office of an elementary school, checking my mail, when suddenly there was a wailing cry. I saw two third-grade girls hurrying down the hall, one had her arm around her sobbing classmate, who had blood dripping down her face and blouse. Her nose was bleeding profusely, and she was obviously scared and hurt. The office manager immediately grabbed a handful of tissues and hurried the girls into the nurse's office. (We had a nurse two days a week.) She was so calm and soothing that within a couple of minutes the girls settled down; I soon heard their giggling. Knowing you could go to the office and be well cared for was like having a security blanket always available. Students and staff knew they could rely on the office manager to be attentive, compassionate, and patient in any situation. She was a valuable asset to the school and also helped foster a positive, nurturing environment.

There are two personnel-related issues that cut across all staff—whether they work in administration, in the classroom, on the playground, or elsewhere—and have a significant impact on school culture. The first is the imbalance of men and women in schools, especially at the elementary level. In my experience at four different elementary schools, there were about twenty-five to forty women on staff versus one to four men (one of which was usually a custodian). In Washington State, over 85 percent of elementary teachers are women.[17] Nationally, approximately 89.5 percent of elementary public-school teachers are women.[18] In part, this stems from an antiquated, sexist belief that teaching children is "women's work" (hence also the requisite lower pay and lack of respect that comes with being a teacher compared to other professions). However, children benefit from having role models who are both male and female—and school culture benefits too, becoming more inclusive and providing a variety of perspectives.

In addition to gender imbalance among staff, there is one other personnel-wide issue that can affect school culture—and that's turnover. If a school is constantly hiring new teachers, if paraprofessionals and other staff are constantly coming and going, then a feeling of uncertainty and apathy can pervade: Why try when you know that so-and-so who is supposed to be in charge is going to be gone quicker than you can snap your fingers? Students learn more effectively and staff tend to be more motivated and inspired in a stable environment, one where you can count on peers and colleagues to lend support and guidance.

Paraprofessionals, volunteers, and other personnel are an integral part of school culture. Some schools have effective, positive staff supporting teachers and students. Interacting with those people may be the highlight of a child's day. When pondering whether students experience success, it helps to consider who it is that spends time with them and the kind of environment they foster.

Community Influences

A school's culture does not exist in a bubble; the values, beliefs, and atmosphere of the students' community have a significant effect on what happens inside classrooms. For example, what are the students' attitudes toward formal education? Do they just want out of high school, or do they think beyond to college or trade schools? Do parents believe their children can go on to higher education, or is it just a pipe dream because of economics? Do the students come ready to learn and get along, or are they more ready to fight authority and their peers?

The answers to those questions give insight into what students bring to school with them every day, and why certain behaviors happen. Students who come with negative attitudes often share those feelings openly and tend to be more defiant and have conflicts with peers and adults. Students who come to school with a thirst for learning and a cooperative attitude will create a whole different atmosphere than students who don't want to learn—or don't think they can learn.

While it is up to school staff to foster a safe environment where curiosity and learning are encouraged, the students and their actions (though influenced by the community) contribute to school culture.

Reflections of School Culture

Seems subtle at first, but as you look closely, you can see and feel a school's culture and how it influences what happens with students. How do you identify a school's culture? There are many questions you can ask whose answers provide clues about a particular school's values and how those values shape the environment. Here are a few examples:

- How many parents are in the PTA?

- Are there lots of volunteers at the school?

- How are families welcomed?

- How do the office staff treat people, and do they seem efficient?

- What kinds of things are emphasized in the communications sent home? Do they focus on the tenants of basic parenting or meaningful ideas on how to help children learn?

- What kinds of things are celebrated at the school—science, music, or merely attendance?

- Do you hear laughter? (A personal belief is that laughter is a sign of people feeling comfortable, and people can achieve more when feeling comfortable.)

- Does the principal encourage and support teachers, or just look at test scores?

- What are the demographics of the teaching staff?

- What is the staff turnover?

- What kinds of attitudes are prevalent among staff?

- What are the demographics of the student body?

- What is emphasized in classrooms?

- Is there consistency among classrooms and grades?

- Do the actions of administration and teachers seem to match words most of the time? (Do they walk their talk?)

The answers to the questions listed above can reflect the day-to-day experiences of students and to what extent they can focus on learning. In addition to asking the right questions, there are three aspects of school life that are also very telling about culture: assemblies, special events, and staff rooms.

Kickoff Assemblies

The school intercom crackles to life: "Our first assembly of the year starts in ten minutes. All primary classes need to leave now. Intermediate classes will *walk* to the assembly in five minutes."

Rules, rules, and more rules are emphasized at the beginning of the school year, even as adults express hope and excitement. There's definitely an art to delivering both of these messages to children without having them seem at odds. It's so easy, as an adult, to forget how smart children are and how quickly they sense consistency and sincerity. We tend to underestimate them, assuming way too much about what they've "forgotten" over the summer. Nevertheless, a check-in is always necessary.

Most schools kick off the year with an assembly during the first week of classes. It's one way to reinforce school-wide rules while also fostering enthusiasm among the students and staff. These assemblies can be fun and invigorating or boring and chaotic. As teachers usher students to their seats, one can often hear, "Shh—hands and feet to yourself," "Walk in a straight line," or "Sit with your rear on the floor— crisscross applesauce."

Observing five hundred or more children filing into an assembly and sitting on hard floors for up to forty-five minutes with varying degrees of participation is quite revealing about a school's culture: Do the children know where to sit and how to behave appropriately? Are teachers constantly having to discipline students, or—at the other extreme—do they just let disruption happen? How do teachers keep it together? With a look, a nod of the head, or maybe a snap of the fingers? Or do voices have to come into play and how loud? Once the assembly starts, how does the principal or whomever is running the assembly set the tone? Is that tone caring, with clear directions and expectations, or is it muddled? Is there a power struggle just to get kids to stand and recite the Pledge of Allegiance? Children need guidelines and structure, and I've seen both ends of the spectrum—from a great "family" experience to a gathering of wild cats.

Teacher skits about school-wide rules and how to handle particular situations often appear in beginning-of-the-year assemblies. But even if the information is communicated clearly, either through skit or direct address, kids will still be kids. Students may remember the humorous moments of those teacher skits ("You were funny when you dropped your books as you ran, Mr. Green!"), but the rules will often be broken. Usually the general message, which isn't rocket science (e.g., "We always walk in the hall"), is necessary, and yet there is a need to repeat the expectations often and to follow through on enforcing them. Too often adults think that just telling children once will make a lasting impact. Or conversely, rules are repeated more than anything else in the school day, so children tend to mimic and ignore them. It can be tricky to set a clear expectation (and reinforce it) without belaboring the issue. What is often forgotten or not emphasized enough is what happens *preceding* a rule infraction and how a positive and safe school climate can prevent many issues before they start.

One principal at a school my daughters attended was particularly skilled at engaging students during assemblies. It was a tough school, and he decided to hold short, weekly assemblies just to set the tone for each week. During each assembly, he would ask, "How's your attitude?" And the students would respond in unison: "Positive!" They had been coached from the start of the year to say this, and week after week you could tell from their shouting that they *were* excited and sincere. He was genuine and present with the children, kept his promises, and consistently addressed discipline issues. Behavior problems went way down, academic achievement and attendance went up, and teachers were happier. Weekly assemblies were just one of the tools this principal used to foster a school culture that was orderly, upbeat, and respectful.

One school where I worked set a much different tone at the beginning of the year, and as a result had a much different culture. There were two school rules I heard repeated ad nauseam: "Make sure you put your name in the top right corner of your paper with the date and your student number," and "Line up in a straight line, tuck in your shirts, and no talking." While following these instructions was important, they were emphasized to the point where little else seemed to matter. Yes, students need to walk as a class from one place to another without chaos taking over, yet to have so much time and effort put into maintaining straight, disciplined lines seems almost military-like. And yes, putting names on papers is also essential, yet again, following this small procedure shouldn't overshadow the content children are producing. "I won't even look at this until you put your name, date, and student number in the proper place." That statement from a third-grade teacher doesn't seem to foster an atmosphere of inquiry. It's more about exercising control—training children to be followers.

What routines are in place, what is emphasized regularly, as well as what adults say and how they act are part of what establishes a school's culture. Positivity and enthusiasm are just as contagious as bad attitudes. Each year is an opportunity to establish a learning environment with clear and reasonable expectations for how to function in the school. Assemblies and special events are a way to demonstrate and celebrate what is valued.

Special Events

Schools bring students together throughout the year for various reasons—to learn about fire prevention or celebrate Black History Month, for example. There are often gatherings to acknowledge holidays such as Veterans Day, Memorial Day, and Martin Luther King Jr. Day. And most schools hold award ceremonies at the end of the year. Assemblies that feature music, storytelling, and science—and have meaningful connections to what children value—can be beneficial. Feeling it was important to have purposeful yet fun gatherings throughout the year that made use of community resources, I gladly accepted the duty of directing the Assembly Committee (of which I was the only member) for seven years at one school where I worked.

Some special assemblies didn't work as well as others. For example, once I had over five hundred children waiting in the gym and the presenter I'd lined up never showed or called. Bless the music teacher who led the school in songs before we gave up and went back to class. However, most of what I arranged went well, from science experiments with safe explosions to music that made the children sway and bop while delivering messages of peace and justice. Breaking up the routine with a few meaningful assemblies can provide special memories for children and reinforce ideas. Also, there is nothing wrong with a little fun in life.

My friend Kevin, who helped my students and me produce the film about Ryan White, and his wife, Susanne, ran a nonprofit that put on educational science assemblies. They would get students and adults so enthusiastic that science experiments would frequently spring up in classrooms—working with magnets and electricity or experimenting with dry ice. (It didn't hurt that Kevin and Suzanne would start small fires or make things "magically" move across the gym.)

Other special events that helped foster a sense of community showcased the students themselves. Choir and band concerts offered wonderful opportunities for students to perform and learn the importance of practice. Many students like to be in the limelight and will do well if given the chance. For example, the annual assembly for Martin Luther King Jr. Day (a significant event at the diverse schools where I taught) would often feature students reading essays, singing songs, or performing skits.

Some gatherings I arranged were just for having fun and enhancing camaraderie. For example, staff versus student athletic events were great hits. (I still remember playing softball when I was in sixth grade myself and how amazed I was that teachers could run!) The excitement of a few hundred children cheering their peers and teachers brought everyone together like a family. The years I was teaching elementary school, I was able to talk the staff I worked with into three events (as long as I did the arranging, most of them were happy to support the effort): volleyball in the fall, basketball in late winter, and softball in the late spring. Those events became part of that school's culture, and the students anticipated them every year.

The sixth graders, the oldest students, played against the staff. Logistically it was a bit complex preventing students from whining about not playing enough. The eighty or so sixth graders were told they had a choice between either volleyball or basketball, and everyone could play softball if they wanted. After a bit of "Aw, man!" moaning, they all realized it was the fairest way to ensure everyone who wanted to play could. Not all sixth-grade students wanted to participate. Those that didn't often helped monitor younger children whose teachers were playing (another positive community-building result). The games were lively and smiles abounded. Score was loosely kept, though lots of talk about it after was all in fun. "*We* won Mr. Green—the scorekeeper cheated." And younger students often looked forward to playing too. "Just wait until I'm in sixth grade—we will beat you then!" I heard that from all ages, especially the fifth graders.

Some adults were enthusiastic about the games and enjoyed the challenge, while others took a little prodding to participate. Some were not into it at all as they feared embarrassment. Thus I often had to recruit a parent or two to fill out the staff squads. Some adults were vocal about it not getting too competitive: "We are all winners." Others were just as passionate about winning: "There is no way those kids are going to win!"

The games gave adults and students an opportunity to come together as a community. Many adults pitched in to help make the games happen. For example, PE teachers taught whatever sport we were going to play in class around the time of the event to increase success, and some served as referees or played as well. The students always got a big kick out of seeing adults in athletic clothing. (My students were so used to me being in a coat and tie that seeing me in shorts was quite a shock: "You have legs!") A big moment was when the principal would play. (It is challenging for some children to understand how teachers and principals are capable of playing beyond their roles inside school.) With few exceptions, the children behaved well while watching the games; they knew it was a special gig, so they lived up to expectations. Plus, it was an opportunity to holler without getting in trouble. I received many positive comments about the events over the years and heard many students reminisce about the games they played or watched. (Some parents thought the games were so meaningful that years later one mother was still upset that her usually well-behaved son missed out on the basketball game due to his involvement in a minor food-throwing incident during lunch!)

The reasons that schools bring students together provide a window into the culture. Events are one indication of how much a school values camaraderie and community. Breaking up routines with a special event allows students and teachers to interact with people within the school they may not connect with on a regular basis. Seeing adults in different contexts like pitching a softball or dribbling down a basketball court reveals the humanity of the staff—reminds the students that we are regular people (who have legs!), which enhances the learning environment. Whether it is a gathering to learn about science, celebrate reading, or play softball, assemblies and special events remind children they are part of a community that values them.

Staff Rooms

Staff rooms can also reflect the attitudes of a school. Some are warm and friendly, while others are cold and impersonal. Of particular note is how staff rooms are maintained and who spends time there. Are they filled with signs like "Your mother doesn't work here; clean up your mess"? Do people label everything in the refrigerator, or is there trust and sharing? Does everyone go in there to eat or just a few cliques? Are substitutes welcomed into conversations? The actual content of the conversations is perhaps the most telling. Do you hear complaints often? Is there genuine laughter? How much talk is focused on the exciting things students are doing versus their bad behavior? Do staff members talk about other adults in a positive or negative light? (Of course, every now and then a healthy purging of frustrations can be useful.)

Some teachers avoid staff rooms and interactions with colleagues because of the negative conversations (which they themselves may hold in other places) that often occur there. I usually ate in the staff room, though sometimes I left mid-lunch, wondering why I spent my precious twenty minutes of free time immersed in complaints about students, administration, politics, spouses, and life in general. When fellow staff weren't venting, the discussion often revolved around topics I had no interest in at all.

Schools where adults get along, actually enjoy interacting with each other—often in the staff room—tend to be better places for students. Cliques are hard to avoid in any setting, and it is unreasonable to expect everyone to like each other. However, adults who display good leadership and share the common goal of educating children can make great progress in establishing a positive workplace.

A school's culture has many facets and is often obvious if you know what to look for—student behavior in assemblies, any special events the school promotes, and the types of extracurricular activities offered, for example. No two schools are exactly alike, which is part of why just replicating a strategy for student success most likely won't work. Individual school cultures are influenced heavily by the communities they serve, which each have their own intricacies. It's important to maintain a balance between rolling out big ideas in schools across the board and allowing for differences in implementation. (For example, it doesn't have to be chess or music, but something for the school to rally around is key.) In Chapter 8, we'll explore how community values affect schools.

Chapter 8

Community Culture: What Outside Forces Affect Student Learning?

Communities Permeate Classrooms

Most years, without fail, a common situation in class would unfold like this:

One boy elbows his neighbor who is working on an assignment. "Man, why do you always do the extra work? What are you trying to prove?"

The instigator's buddy adds, "Yeah, you act like you like schoolwork!"

I intervene because the student being targeted would often turn red and clam up. "So gentlemen, do you know what you call an adult nerd or geek?"

The boys shake their heads no while the rest of the class looks up. "You call them boss!" I exclaim with a smile. The teasers shrink just a little, and you can tell they are thinking about what I said. Most of the class chuckles and then gets back to their assignment (though, sometimes an explanation is necessary).

This interaction is indicative of how aspects of community culture, in this case negative attitudes about working hard in school, show up in classrooms. Similar to how school culture influences student achievement, community culture—the values, beliefs, behaviors, and attitudes of the public—have a significant impact on student success and daily life in schools. Communities exist on a national, regional, and local level—and the cultural dynamics of each affect what goes on in classrooms. For example, a cynical attitude about intellectual pursuits is a national sentiment.

Schools and districts mirror the economic and ethnic diversity of their communities, and they also reflect the social issues these communities face, from anti-intellectualism to social injustice. For example, poverty disproportionally affects people of color. In the United States, 39 percent of African American children and 33 percent of Latino children are living in poverty, while the poverty rate for white and Asian children is only 14 percent.[19]

That economic inequality is reflected in what's known as the "achievement gap" in schools—the disparity in academic performance between certain groups of students. Black, Latino, and Native American students historically don't perform as well as their white or Asian peers. For decades, students of color have been underrepresented in gifted programs and higher mathematics and sciences, while they tend to overpopulate remedial classes and special education programs. Many fail to graduate on time—or at all.

Data from the 2016–17 school year in Washington State shows that about 82 percent of white students and 88 percent of Asian students graduate on time (in four years), while only about 72 percent of Blacks and 73 percent of Hispanics graduate on time. Sixty percent of American Indians make it through high school with their peers.[20] Nationally, graduation rates are similar, though slightly higher. (See table 8.1.)

2015–16 Public High School Graduation Rates	
Race	Percentage of Students Who Graduated Within Four Years
White	88%
Black	76%
Asian	91%
Hispanic	79%
American Indian / Alaska Native	72%

Source: National Center for Education Statistics, "Public High School Graduation Rates," May 2018, https://nces.ed.gov/programs/coe/indicator_coi.asp.

Another example of a community issue that is reflected in classrooms across the country is the disproportionate number of people of color who are policed and incarcerated. In the United States, Black and Hispanic people make up about 32 percent of the total population, yet 56 percent of those in prison.[21] This problem also manifests in schools through the frequency with which some students are reprimanded. For example, Black students in Seattle Public Schools were suspended or expelled at five times the rate of white students in the 2012–13 school year. Another large district, thirty miles south of Seattle, suspended 16 percent of Black students for at least a day compared to 5 percent of white students and 3 percent of Asian students.[22]

We can whittle away at school reform all we want; however, until systemic community issues, such as racism, poverty, and violence, are meaningfully addressed, many students will continue to struggle academically. After all, can you expect children to focus on homework if their home life isn't stable? If they're wondering whether they will have anything to eat for dinner, if Dad got arrested again, or if the drug dealer on the corner is going to harass them on the way to school? Intellectual endeavors will take a back seat to survival. And intellectual endeavors are already endangered.

Anti-Intellectualism

One large obstacle to quality public education in the United States is the lack of value our culture places on intellect. This is nothing new. Richard Hofstadter's book *Anti-intellectualism in American Life*, published in the early 1960s, chronicles how our country has a history of scorning intellect, a phenomenon that stems from a desire to differentiate ourselves from the European "elite." Our nation's Christian roots, which tend to value conviction over education, faith over curiosity, also have a part to play.

This hostile relationship with intellect can be traced back to the way people viewed some of the founding fathers. For example, Thomas Jefferson was a key figure in our independence yet he was ridiculed because of his university education; it was considered a reason he could not relate to the average citizen, though he wrote that all men are created equal. (Of course, it was still only white men with property who could vote at that time. Gender, racial, and economic disparities separated people then also.) Hofstadter also cites how popular evangelists like Billy Sunday in the early 1900s said, "The only book worth reading is the good book!" (meaning the Bible). To believe otherwise was a ticket straight to hell. Even universities founded by the church had controversies over the teaching of ideas that might contradict the messages in the Bible, most obviously evolution. During the presidential campaigns of the 1950s, candidate Adlai Stevenson II was scoffed at for being too intellectual and detached from the "common man." Many lauded Eisenhower because "common sense," which he used successfully as a general in World War II, was considered more valuable than intellect.

The push against intellectualism hasn't abated. Two-term president George W. Bush was touted as someone you would want to have a beer with, a man of the people, whereas his opponents, both Al Gore and John Kerry, were depicted as too scholarly and detached. The "tradition" of ridiculing those who are formally educated stems from the fact that for generations most people could not afford higher education, creating a perceived sharp divide between social classes. "Book-smart" people were—and continue to be—accused of being elitist and mucking up clear-cut issues with ideas and questions.

Consider how common it is for people to buy into simplistic solutions to complicated issues:
"You are either with us or against us."
"Just put a fence up on the border."
"We need to test them to see if they are ready for the *big* test."
"If we all used positive discipline (or this math text or that reading program), then students would excel."

In-depth intellectual discussions that get into the gray areas of reality are rarely encouraged in mainstream culture, and thus difficult to pull off in the classroom. Students tend to mimic the adults in their lives, spouting bumper-sticker solutions instead of asking questions, listening to others, and engaging in thoughtful analysis. Looking at issues like racism or ecology from multiple perspectives is harder when popular culture, thanks in large part to the rise of social media, tends to worship at the altar of the 280-character message.

Another aspect of our culture that feeds anti-intellectualism is the way we value entertainment over education. How many people read Hollywood gossip, watch reality TV, or obsess over sports versus the number of people who read books, study the newspaper, or research a topic they know nothing about? If we valued education, wouldn't it be unthinkable to have situations like in Portland, Oregon, in 2003, when they cut the school year three weeks short due to lack of money?[23] Would we let children attend classes in buildings that have lead in the water, are filled with asbestos, and aren't safe from earthquakes or other natural occurrences?[24] Wouldn't teachers be looked at with the same awe as athletes and movie stars? Would we accept the realities of budget cuts that eliminate programs like all-day kindergarten or make teachers spend their own money for basic supplies like paper and pencils?

Our values and priorities as a nation are a major reason why public schools struggle financially and student achievement languishes: the pursuit of knowledge for its own sake is not something all Americans value. However, the real danger goes beyond poor test scores, for without people who have developed intellectual habits of mind— listening with empathy, engaging in flexible thinking, questioning one's beliefs,[25] for example—we will never rectify other social ills like racism and poverty.

Racism

Racism is a social justice issue that pervades both communities and schools. For example, a Black or Hispanic male who engages in mouthy, defiant behavior will typically get suspended or booted from class: "He just won't listen—he's very disrespectful." However, a white girl who behaves in the same way is often reprimanded but not kicked out: "She just gets a little wound up and needs a reminder."

Perhaps where racism is most readily apparent is in the makeup and treatment of gifted programs (a.k.a., "highly capable programs"). While working as a mathematics coach at a school, I had an experience that is unfortunately common across many classrooms. The school was ethnically diverse, with about 75 percent of students receiving free or reduced lunch prices. There were two to three regular education classes for each grade level, and many students were in the special education program. There was one "gifted" class in the school populated by twenty-three third-, fourth- and fifth-grade students. My job was to support instruction by modeling lessons and doing staff development. One day, the class was working in table groups and I was about to model a math lesson for the teacher using a story. The teacher, who didn't seem comfortable having someone else lead her class, was tense as she asked the students to clear their desks and get ready for my lesson. She hovered anxiously on the side of the classroom.

"I'm going to read this book out loud, and you are to listen for how math plays a part in the story," I said. "I will stop a couple of times and pose a problem from the information in the book." As I read, the children were listening well, a couple of them doodling (which I didn't mind at all). One boy was resting his cheek on the desk as he doodled aimlessly. Yet he responded to a question I asked, showing he was paying attention. No problem for me.

About five minutes into the lesson, suddenly the teacher blurted out, "I said sit up!" I froze. The doodlers who had their heads on their arms also sat up, but breathed a sigh of relief when they realized the teacher wasn't speaking to them. The teacher was looming over one child (who happened to be one of two Black children in the class). "I've told you, you need to sit up and pay attention!" she barked.

I'm thinking, *He is paying attention—didn't you hear him respond?* But instead I said, "It's okay. I know he's listening."

"I just can't have that kind of behavior in class, Mr. Green. This isn't the first time." Then she walked him down to the principal's office. I went on with the lesson with a heavy heart.

She later came to me and said he was a constant behavior problem and she couldn't wait to get him out of her class. "Besides he isn't gifted anyway—he's just there because he's Black."

Whoa, I didn't just hear that, I thought. I said I was sorry he was a problem for her, but I thought he understood the lesson. She continued to grumble about him being disruptive and not belonging in her class, at which point I chose not to pursue the matter anymore. I'm fairly sure she didn't realize her bigotry. She, like many people, had a preset notion about what a gifted student was like, and this child didn't fit in her head.

What *does* it mean to be gifted or highly capable? There is a lot of controversy about who gets into these programs, how much weight recommendations carry, and how students are screened. Some educators mistake hard work and good behavior for giftedness. Some gifted students misbehave and do not work hard due to boredom or lack of interest, not lack of intelligence. Rather than sit idly and sneak in a pleasure book or *Mad* magazine, these students may challenge the teacher, flirt with other students, or crack jokes, behavior that gets in the way of everyone's learning. Yet rather than looking to engage those students in appropriate academic challenges, teachers often get into power struggles. The unfortunate end result of this issue is that the demographics of gifted classes don't come close to being equitable in many communities. (See table 8.2.)

Washington State Fifth Graders Enrolled in Highly Capable (HC) Program, 2017–18 School Year			
Race	Total Number of Fifth Graders	Number of Fifth Graders in HC Program	Percentage of Fifth Graders in HC Program
Hispanic/Latino	21,266	543	2.5%
American Indian / Alaska Native	1,135	23	2%
Asian	6,456	1,136	17.5%
Black / African American	3,729	124	3.3%
Native Hawaiian / Other Pacific Islander	984	14	1.4%
White	46,120	4,086	8.8%
Two or More Races	7,470	595	7.9%
Race Not Provided	5	N/A	N/A
Total	87,165	6,521	N/A

Note: Eighty percent of fifth graders enrolled in the HC program were white or Asian. The idea is ludicrous that, among Washington State fifth graders, almost one in five Asian students is "gifted" versus only about one out of thirty Black students.

Sources: First column: Comprehensive Education Data and Research System (CEDARS), demographic data about enrollment in elementary gifted programs, accessed August 30, 2018, http://www.k12.wa.us/CEDARS/default.aspx; second column: data from OSPI HCP Office; third column: self-calculated.

For example, Miami-Dade County public schools found that the makeup of their gifted programs did not reflect school demographics. As a result, they decided to change their screening process; rather than relying only on results from an IQ test (which has been found to be culturally biased), they examined other factors such as creativity and academic achievement to determine if a child is gifted. They also took into account that even highly intelligent students can have gaps in academic success or misbehave. Since 2007, they have funneled significant money and resources into making gifted classes more representative of the overall student population, which it now is.[26] (See table 8.3.)

Makeup of Miami-Dade County's Gifted Program		
Race	Percentage of Gifted Program	Percentage of District
White	16.1%	7.1%
Black	13.8%	21.1%
Asian	2.5%	1.1%
Hispanic	66.5%	70.1%

Source: Claudia Rowe, "The Push to Find More Gifted Kids: What Washington Can Learn from Miami's Wins," Seattle Times, December 7, 2017, https://www.seattletimes.com/education-lab/the-push-to-find-more-gifted-kids-what-washington-can-learn-from-miamis-wins/?utm_source=marketingcloud&utm_medium=email&utm_campaign=Ed+Lab+12.7.17_12_7_2017.

The unbalanced makeup of students in gifted courses sometimes keeps students who should be in those classes away. Carlos, a bright eighth grader I worked with, didn't like the teachers or other students in the gifted program. "I just can't relate to those spoiled kids," he told me. He was Hispanic and his family did not have much money, while the majority of students in the gifted program were white and more financially comfortable. Though he should have been in algebra, where the other "gifted" students were placed, he was in my pre-algebra class. Carlos understood the concepts and was able to apply them quickly—that is, if he didn't already know how to do the problems. Sometimes he would even do extra credit work I offered. He never misbehaved and often helped his classmates, who liked him.

Carlos missed a whole week of school once, which puzzled me. I then heard from the vice principal that he'd been suspended for hacking into the district's computer system and changing his grades. When I asked him about it, he said, "I was bored one night, Mr. Green. It really was pretty easy." There is no guarantee he wouldn't have done it even if he had been more appropriately challenged among a group of students he could relate to, but his intelligence was certainly not engaged at school. I'm not sure what happened to him, but I hope he found a niche where he could be happy and make good use of his intellect.

Racism is a community issue that negatively affects minority populations on a national scale in the United States. It permeates decisions and interactions in public schools at every level. Students, who (like anyone) want to fit in with their peers, notice who is in which classes. They notice who gets kicked out or suspended and who doesn't. They notice whom teachers call on, whom they ignore, and whom they single out for reprimands. We—school leaders, parents, and educators—should take notice, too, and ask ourselves why some students are treated a particular way while others are not. Unfortunately, many students who must live with the consequences of racism in the community and classroom also suffer from poverty.

Poverty

It's 7:30 a.m. and twenty-five students are waiting to go into the cafeteria (a.k.a. gym/assembly area) for breakfast. Within ten minutes another 150 or so students join them to eat a "healthy" meal of two pieces of "French toast" that look like two plump French fries, a small plastic cup of syrup, a cup of peaches in some sort of liquid, milk (maybe chocolate milk), and a sausage patty that resembles a hockey puck. (Have you ever tried to use a spork to eat a sausage patty that could break windows?) The children who try to use the flimsy spork to cut the sausage are frustrated when the cheap plastic bends and snaps in two. Many just stab at the patty with similar results. Most children eat the French toast and some of the peaches, and the brave ones just pick up the sausage and chomp on it. They are obviously hungry.

Many families rely on meal programs at school to feed their children. For example, in 2017, 42.9 percent of all Washington State students received free or reduced-price meals.[27] (Some summer school programs even feed children who are not enrolled due to need.) These meals supposedly represent "balanced nutrition." I'm not sure who really checks that or how it is determined, yet I am glad I don't have to rely on those meals for sustenance. I doubt the inspectors eat the stuff, at least not every day. Over my teaching career, the quality of the food was such that I observed many children skipping breakfast or picking at the meals, only to supplement with something like a bag of Flamin' Hot Cheetos they somehow obtained. (No offense to the people who prepare the food. They do the best they can given strict guidelines and limited resources.)

Long gone are the days when school meals were actually cooked at individual schools. Early in the morning, a district's central kitchens prepare meals that are placed in plastic trays. These trays are stacked in warmers, loaded onto trucks, and delivered to the schools. By the time the meals are rolled off the trucks into the cafeterias, where students line up hoping to fill their stomachs, it's typically been several hours after the food was originally placed on the plastic trays. No wonder a bag of Cheetos seems like the preferable option.

A good diet is important to a healthy mind. While there are programs and schools where fresh vegetables and fruit are served, some even grown on-site, it is still rare, especially in high-poverty schools (where I saw a couple of the nastiest salad bars—wilting lettuce, brown broccoli, flies hovering—that few brave souls will pick at). Many children count on school meals, and the schools with higher free or reduced-meal rates have, in general, the most issues with behavior and attendance. Seems like we write off children for the sake of money spent in other ways. If just 10 percent of the money spent on hot-air political campaigns, for example, went toward feeding needy children, the quality of food could go up substantially. That would be over $600 million from the 2016 elections (over $6.8 billion spent).[28]

As a teacher, I found it difficult to ignore the poor nutrition in school meals. It was part of why I started bringing apples to class, instead of giving out candy—which I did my share of—as a reward. Some students would ask me for a second or third apple. I regret not doing that more. I also regret the many times while taking the daily lunch count that I would ask, "How many are eating the school slop, I mean school lunch, today?" A feeble attempt at humor. Everyone knew the food wasn't great, and I hope I didn't make any child feel worse about themselves or their families because that was their only option.

Food is just one aspect of poverty that young people deal with every day—at home and school. A lot of children rely on clothing banks as well (only to be teased mercilessly by peers sometimes). In addition, many immigrant families count on their children to act as interpreters between adults at home and at school, which is unfair. An eight-year-old child shouldn't have to act as a translator so their parents can get information from school about events, the child's own progress, or community services that provide basic necessities. It is too much for a child and difficult for the parents.

High poverty rates within communities are also reflected in the lack of care and equity in school buildings. Many schools are old and unsafe. The amount of temporary portables is just astonishing. Asbestos, faulty wiring, leaky roofs, boilers that break or heat only in the summer, noisy pipes, and undrinkable water are common—and yet we expect children to learn under these conditions.[29] Students can see if things are run-down or not, and some might feel it a reason to not care, while others might be upset knowing that other schools, mostly in affluent areas, have more up-to-date facilities. The derelict state of a school building can be a distraction from learning, which is hard enough under the best conditions, and unfortunately the neighborhood schools that need the most repairs often don't get them.

The effects of poverty extend beyond school facilities to infiltrate classrooms as well. Students may be dealing with a variety of disruption that makes focusing on studies difficult: moving for the third time in eighteen months, relying on school meals for nutrition as discussed earlier, or having to make it through the winter in the same sweater and jacket that have been let out a half dozen times and still are too tight. Knowing a little about the culture of poverty can help teachers work with students. Educator and author Ruby Payne differentiates between situational poverty, where a sudden change like a job loss or illness puts families in need, and generational poverty, where a family has lived in a state of poverty for two generations or longer.[30] Those families in a state of generational poverty don't place the same value on long-term planning and attending college as other people. When all you know is poverty and how quickly things can fall apart, survival mode is primary; relationships and entertainment are valued more than education. After all, they have seen or heard of many instances where it can all end in a moment. College takes a back seat to day-today survival. Topics that are top of mind to children in generational poverty are who is employed today, who is involved in what gang, what bills are stressing Mom and Dad out, and what relatives are dealing with the law. Apathy towards formal education is prevalent in part due to seeing it does not lead to immediate success, and also because college costs are out of the question—and with college being the carrot most often dangled for achieving prosperity, a disconnect is created.

Payne also points out, for instance, that the working vocabulary of many people in generational poverty is around four hundred to eight hundred words—those who don't live in poverty have a vocabulary of about ten times that amount. Families who don't use the language style and structure that is common in business and school can't expose their children to it.

Yet despite the strains poverty places on many children, I am constantly amazed at their resilience and generosity. For example, I have never understood the logic behind canned food drives in schools where 75 percent of the student body is on free or reduced lunch rates, but they were held—with success. And when it was time to give, the kids who needed help themselves would contribute. They just wanted to make the world better.

These are just a few examples of how economic status influences what happens in schools and ultimately affects student achievement. Nutritious food and adequate shelter are basic needs, yet many educators, adults living above the poverty line, policy makers, and politicians worry about test scores. People in poverty don't necessarily think about which colleges their children should visit before applying when they are worried about paying the water bill. Also, violence tends to permeate poorer sections of cities; thus, again, survival becomes more important than, perhaps, reading Shakespeare.

Violence

Nationally, the rate of violent crime has declined significantly over the past two decades, dropping 48 percent between 1993 and 2016.[31] Yet individual neighborhoods, particularly those that are stricken by poverty or heavily populated by minorities, still experience a disproportionate amount of violent crime.[32] Schoolchildren in high-poverty areas are exposed to gang violence, robberies, drug abuse, and shootings, among other brutalities, and their survival seems to depend on toughness. That mind-set spills over into schools, leading to bullying, power struggles with teachers, drug use, and apathy toward learning. (Security guards and metal detectors may increase safety but not necessarily peace of mind to think and learn.) Yet with some concerted effort, school staff can foster safer learning communities, and during my second year teaching at one middle school, I had an opportunity to do just that.

The school abutted a Section 8 housing project and had a poor reputation. About 80 percent of the students lived in poverty, and sixty different languages were spoken in homes, which made communication with families difficult. Gang activity and drug abuse were frequent on school grounds. There was lots of bullying, and I often heard students talk about a fight that was going to happen after school (which I was required to report to office staff who would pass it on to local law enforcement, but it didn't stop the violence). Suspensions and power struggles were common. Many people, students and staff, didn't feel safe there. One day, the new principal approached me about starting a leadership group for students in an effort to get them involved in making the school a safer place focused on learning. The first step was to identify the leaders of the school—not just the high-achieving students, but also the "street leaders," the ones who ran the halls.

The group met during my planning period, so the students missed a class, which many of them thought was great. I tried to get them to embrace their ability to influence others and create a school where everyone felt safe and secure, but the group wasn't coming together. Contrary to what the principal and I hoped, they remained cocooned in the safety of their cliques. Eventually, I contacted the organization Students Against Violence Everywhere, and they put me in contact with a special man whom I invited to speak with the students.

A former member of the Black Panthers, he was tall and good-looking, had a commanding presence, and most important, did not hold back with the students. He spoke of standing on street corners openly carrying firearms because of police brutality, explaining that some gun control laws were enacted in response to Black people standing up to police violence. Yet he was passionate about the truth and how guns and violence were not the answer. He laid into the kids for not knowing about people like Cesar Chavez, Medgar Evers, or Fannie Lou Hamer. He stressed the importance of knowing history to move forward.

He lambasted the street leaders in the group for glorifying "gangsta rap." "No real gangster wants to be seen, let alone on TV. They lay low. Those rap stars are glorifying violence and 'ghetto life' while taking your money and buying Mercedes and gold chains. They are playing you!" he said, urging the students to use their brains and resources to instead make the world better. Some students seemed to understand right away what he was saying, while others looked confused or were perhaps mulling over his message.

When teachers started to complain about students missing a class each week, which I understood, I started meeting with the group after school. Unfortunately, many street leaders chose not to continue, and without their support we did little to change the school at first. But at least some talk was happening among students about the issue of violence and what we could do about it. About ten students attended our weekly meetings with a couple of the street leaders coming by irregularly. Yet we were all determined to make a difference.

When I showed the group an article about some high school students who had painted a mural, graffiti-style, with a message of peace, they were intrigued. The cafeteria at the school had two large murals painted on the walls depicting a scene that could be from *American Graffiti*—smiling white teenagers cruising in old cars to a drive-in burger joint, an image that didn't remotely reflect the student body, considering only 30 percent of the students were white and many lived in poverty. So, with the support of the principal, we decided to paint a peace-themed mural on one of the walls in the cafeteria.

The principal liked the idea and put me in touch with an artist who donated her time. She helped us transform our project from a mere idea depicted on pieces of paper to a twenty-five-by-seven-foot mural on one of the concrete walls. At first, we laid it out on the blackboard in my classroom and then moved into the cafeteria to paint, with all the paint supplies donated by a local hardware store. (It's amazing what people will do for children when asked.) We had to meet on Saturday mornings so classes would not be disrupted and we could spend a few hours working without interruption. The first Saturday we primed the wall and made chalk outlines of our mural. The next two Saturday mornings we painted.

The sight of twelve eighth graders coming to school voluntarily on a Saturday morning to create a peace message was heartwarming. While only a few of them were street leaders, the students were from a mix of backgrounds, reflecting the diversity of the student body. One boy who wore saggy pants that dragged on the ground was artistically talented. I can still recall the image of him holding up his pants with one hand while painting with the other.

The resulting colorful mural brightened up the lunchroom with messages of peace and unity. The style and content were relevant to the children, and while it did not suddenly make everything perfect, it was a step toward a more positive, safe, inclusive school environment.

Perhaps the best part of the whole experience was how students outside the group reacted. The wall we painted was next to the foosball tables, a popular destination during lunch. For three weeks, while we primed, outlined, and painted, the wall was covered with long pieces of butcher paper. Not once did anyone touch it or muck it up—a significant act of restraint for middle schoolers. Word had traveled that this was something students were creating, so it was respected. We had a formal unveiling during lunch to honor the work. The raucous applause felt gratifying.

It's inevitable that issues like violence in the community will affect how classrooms and schools function, but we don't have to throw up our hands and accept it. What kind of message does that send to children? How can we expect them to learn when they don't feel safe? Creating a peace mural was not a panacea for addressing school and community violence, but it was one small step toward creating positive change. If nothing else, it showed the students that the school gave a damn about their well-being, about creating a space free from violence.

Awareness and Tolerance . . . or Lack Thereof

Student populations in the United States are more diverse than ever—and they're only growing more so.[33] Yet many teachers seem unaware of or insensitive to the variety of cultures represented in their classrooms.

Some educators assume that their way of thinking is the same as the families they serve. They make assumptions and judgments about student behavior that are not only false but also create a negative environment. For example, throughout my career I frequently heard teachers saying things like "I need you to look at me so I know you're paying attention," or "One, two, three, eyes on me," yet some Asian cultures believe it is disrespectful to look directly at an authority figure. These same teachers would often call out students who they perceived as too boisterous: "Can you believe how loud Shaniqua is? She just won't lower her volume and is always interrupting. It's just rude!" They didn't take into consideration that Shaniqua and her family were involved in their church, where call-and-response to sermons and spirited vocalization are the norm, not to mention that the girl needed to shout to be heard in her home of seven people.

When some Hispanic students were absent from school for large chunks of time, I often heard statements like "I can't understand why they take off for a month for Christmas. Don't they care about their children's education?" Many immigrants from Mexico and Central America have strong beliefs in the value of family and church, so they go to great lengths to visit loved ones over the holidays, which sometimes lasted much longer than scheduled school vacations. (I used to assign students who traveled "homework" so they would keep up their academic skills. For example, I often asked them to keep a daily diary that tracked numbers such as total miles traveled; average distance covered per day; and the cost of items like milk, bread, and soda pop in different places. Sometimes I also assigned them a book to read.)

Many teachers did not take into account the reality of split families due to immigration laws and economics: "She said she hasn't seen her mother in two years. What kind of mother can do that?" Or: "She told me her uncle sends money to the family every month, and that is why they don't have a computer." Empathy for the obstacles that others face in life doesn't come easily for some. People tend to generalize quickly and judge, without knowing the whole situation.

Taking the time to understand where each child is coming from (even a little bit) and what their family's cultural values are can alleviate misunderstanding and conflict. It also helps establish relationships so the focus is on learning. Some parents may have had bad experiences in school when they were young, and therefore mistrust teachers. Or parents may not know how schools function and thus make their own assumptions. Open communication without judgment fosters understanding and can prevent problems. Building trust between home and school, which comes in part from respecting differences, helps parents and educators support each other in their efforts to help children learn.

Honoring Community Culture

For schools to be positive, safe, and intellectually stimulating places, we must be aware of what life is like within students' communities—what struggles families face; what they value; and how ethnic culture, religion, language, and other characteristics interact to affect student behavior and learning. This is where communication is key—as in most aspects of life, understanding whom you are dealing with can be beneficial to all involved, and one of the ways teachers do that is through conferences with parents, which tend to occur only once or twice a year.

I never understood why parent-teacher contact didn't occur more frequently. Some teachers are just afraid of parents, and many parents think that no news is good news. Perhaps there's just too much assuming on both sides about what's happening and what the reactions might be. Some teachers put out weekly newsletters as a way to keep families updated about what goes on in the classroom. But that is only one-way communication. I looked forward to meeting parents; I gained a lot of insight about my students that way.

Here are some actual statements made at parent conferences:
"I never liked math either."
"I always liked science."
"If you ever have a problem, call me and I'll whup him."
"I can't get him to turn off the TV at night."
"She reads constantly and is always yelling at us to be quiet."
"I get home from work at nine o'clock and they are all supposed to be ready for bed. But my neighbor lets them stay up."

These statements were telling about children's lives. I could understand, for example, why a child was tired or loved science; I learned more about the whole person, which in turn helped me know what kind of support a student needed.

While parent-teacher conferences were invaluable, scheduling them was not easy. In general, I found parents' work schedules prohibitive to conferences. Many simply could not take the time off to attend meetings. Most teachers would do what they could to be accommodating—holding conferences before school or later in the evening, or even conducting conferences over the phone. But sometimes none of those options would work. I often heard teachers saying things like "If they can't take twenty minutes to talk to me, then too bad. I don't have the time to cater to them." It's an attitude I understand—teachers already have enough on their plates without having to chase down parents—but in the end it's the students who suffer when teachers and parents don't communicate. Plus, you never know what's going on beneath the surface. For example, many parents in poverty did not have positive school experiences. So even though they may want to support their child's education, communicating with teachers, walking down a hall, or sitting at a school desk for a meeting can stir up unpleasant memories. Thus, the effort may not be there to show up.

Face-to-face contact with parents was important to me, so for those parents who were unable to make it to conferences at school, I offered to go to their homes in the evening when they returned from work. It was not convenient and kept me away from my own family, yet I learned much about the dynamics of a student's household and community.

Many colleagues were reluctant to visit students' homes. I heard teachers say things like "I don't get paid enough to go to their homes. I have a home, too," or "I won't go there—that whole complex is full of criminals!"

It was true that many of the students I taught over the years lived in areas where unsavory activities flourished, but if that was home to my students, then I felt obliged to go there. There was one apartment complex in particular where I stuck out like a sore thumb (white male in a coat and tie). One day while getting out of my car, I heard a voice say, "Don't worry, Mr. Green, we got your car, man." A scruffy eight-year-old and his grinning four-year-old brother proceeded to lean against the trunk of my used car. Though break-ins, drug dealing, and vandalism were common there, or so I had heard, sure enough, when I returned my car was just as I had left it. Even people involved in criminal activity can value education.

I was a minor celebrity in homes, treated to great food, tea, and coffee by parents and sheepish giggles by children. But most important, those visits provided valuable insight into students' lives; after all, homes are microcosms of the community. For example, I visited one girl's family to see why she had trouble complying with the school's reading program, which required students to read for twenty minutes every day at home.

I discovered my twelve-year-old student lived in a two-bedroom apartment with four other kids and two adults. As soon as I entered, one source of her troubles was clear—noise. The TV was blaring in the living room, where two young children watched an animated show. When I asked if we could turn it off to lessen the distraction during our discussion, my student's mother said, "Oh, it's always on. I've gotten used to it, and the children complain when they can't watch it." Meanwhile, a radio is blaring music from the bathroom, where another child was doing her best rendition of Madonna, and I could also hear TVs booming from the two bedrooms.

Amid coffee and cake, I sat down with the girl's parents to figure out how we could ensure her reading got done. We ended up planning a half hour every day where the TVs were turned off and she got a bedroom to herself to read. Though it didn't work every night, the girl did get more reading time and earned good grades all year. Visiting her home was well worth the time.

Going the extra mile to meet with parents face-to-face who were unable to make it to regular conferences not only helped me to understand a student's social milieu but also helped me to form alliances with parents. I was able to prevent many minor issues, like talking too much in class, from blowing up into major conflicts. When I communicated with parents regularly, they could reinforce expectations at home—"You know Mr. Green expects you to read twenty minutes a day"—and could also help with assignments. When students knew that I had established a relationship with their parents, often a subtle nudge was all that was needed to correct misbehavior: "Now, I know your father would not like that," or "Maybe I should call your momma and have a chat?" Children bring their communities with them when they pass through the school doors, and we—teachers and administrators—cannot effectively help them learn without attempting to understand who they are outside of the classroom.

What Communities Value Shows Up in Schools

Communities affect how well schools function: they are responsible for electing leadership (school boards), interpreting assessment results, selecting content (through the school board), supporting—or not supporting—teachers, and valuing education. Without community support, schools do not flourish. So how can you tell what communities value, or how they feel, in general, about public education? One indicator is what gets publicized. For example, do schools receive positive press for anything besides sports, perhaps for winning academic competitions or performing community service? Another is whether electorates consistently support schools by voting in favor of bond measures. If bonds consistently fail, it can give children a sense that school isn't important—and they do pay attention, particularly when their facilities are old and crumbling, their computers are outdated, or their music program gets cut. A third indicator is the number of volunteers from the community who show up in classrooms and, lastly, whether *all* the schools in a particular area receive equitable support.

While most communities will say they value education, it is in action that the inequities become clear—a school in an affluent neighborhood can have updated technology in all classrooms while a school just a few miles away in a poorer area has one computer lab with fifteen desktops that may or may not crash at any moment. Inequities like this demonstrate a commitment to educating *some* children—those lucky enough to live in wealthy neighborhoods. The question is, are we satisfied with this? If not, if we proclaim to want high-quality education for *all* children, then we must think carefully and holistically about how to proceed. There are steps we can take now while also planning for a more equitable future for all children.

Chapter 9

What Can We Do Now?

Seven Generations

There is a philosophy—attributed to indigenous tribes such as the Iroquois—known as the seventh generation principle. It requires one to abandon self-interest by considering how a decision made today might affect those born seven generations into the future. It's a brilliant model for sustainability, yet one that is rarely applied to any area of American life, much less public education. But it's not too late to take a hard look at how we live, to consider the major influences on a child's educational journey, and start making decisions that will benefit future generations of children—and perhaps even children now.

An easy place to start is adopting the belief that *all* children can learn, that each one has innate talent to be tapped, skills to be fostered, and intellect to cultivate. It costs *nothing* to believe that all children can succeed academically. It costs nothing to believe that the leaders and innovators of tomorrow can come from any neighborhood, be any gender, belong to any race. We must actively dismantle the structure that accepts less than the best for minority children and those living in poverty. To put it bluntly, having family money or white skin does not make one human being more important than another—and it's not enough to just say it. Our actions must support this belief.

Every child deserves the best—so says Article IX of the preamble to the Washington State Constitution (other state constitutions make similar proclamations): "It is the paramount duty of the state to make ample provision for the education of all children residing within its borders, without distinction or preference on account of race, color, caste, or sex."

Sounds great but we are not doing enough to fulfill this duty, as evidenced by disparities in graduation rates and the achievement gap. And we cannot leave it to politicians and educators to do all the work; people from all walks of life could get involved, those who experienced academic success and those who didn't, those who are parents and those who are simply concerned about the state of education in this country.

The first eight chapters of this book aimed to provide you with a foundation of knowledge about the major influences on student learning. Now it's time to consider how to put that information to work so that all children can succeed. This chapter provides an overview about how to make a positive difference, whether it's attending a school board meeting or staying abreast of your school district's policies. I also offer ideas that challenge the status quo of education with the hope of sparking informed discussion about school reform and prompting wise decisions that consider what is best for all children, generations down the line.

Parent Participation

There are steps that any parent can take to fight for equity in the system and help children strive for academic success. You can become as informed and as involved as time permits, and perhaps the best place to begin is the classroom itself.

Establish Good Communication

When students know parents and teachers are in regular contact, they are more likely to succeed. First, it shows that a child's caregivers are invested in their education. Second, children tend to be more honest about what's going on. (It's hard for Junior to lie about doing his homework when he knows Mom and teacher are allies.) Third, communication between parents, teachers, and administration can be productive for reaching a common understanding about academic goals and how to meet them. Teachers learn more about the whole child, and parents get the scoop about classroom activity, expectations, and behavior.

Most educators welcome parental involvement. Parents can and *should* ask questions and then listen to the responses. "What are you doing to help my child meet or exceed learning standards?" and "How can we support my child's learning together?" are examples of what any parent or guardian should feel free to ask teachers. Parents can also ask how to help their child excel in a specific subject like mathematics or why a particular book has been assigned. Open communication can help if there is something a parent doesn't understand about a particular assignment or if the amount of homework seems excessive. Parents should ask administrators how they are keeping students safe in halls and on the playground. Administrators can also address school-wide practices and concerns, such as why cursive writing isn't taught or why students aren't (or are) required to wear uniforms.

Some parents may feel reluctant to get involved, perhaps due to unpleasant childhood experiences in the classroom, time constraints, or financial issues. However, helping children succeed in school is one of the most important responsibilities a parent has. Asking questions, advocating for children's needs, and collaborating with school staff will give students a much better chance of academic achievement. Educators should not only respect parental inquiries and respond appropriately but also encourage more communication.

Educate Yourself

Staying abreast of what's happening in classrooms can put you in the best position to advocate for children's needs as well as meaningful change in the system. You can learn a lot about districts and individual schools online. School websites often have information about educational goals, achievements, student demographics, and messages from the principal (which can be revealing about a school's culture). District websites often contain financial reports, details about instructional materials, policies and procedures, and how the district is organized. This information can reveal what's going well within a school or district and what problems need to be solved. It's a useful jumping-off point for further involvement.

Attend School Board Meetings

School boards serve as the voice of the community, and their decisions have far-reaching effects on students and families, thus parental input is vital. If you want to learn more about district policies or influence decision-making, then consider attending school board meetings, which typically occur once a month. (If scheduling doesn't make that possible, there are usually audio or video recordings of the proceedings available online.)

School board members are responsible for following state education laws and making decisions about how schools in their district operate. They hire superintendents who implement board policies and directives; for example, what resources, including textbooks, teachers must use or whether there are music programs in elementary schools. By attending school board meetings, you can learn firsthand about the decisions they are making and why, share your concerns, and ask questions. You may even become inspired to run for a seat on the board yourself!

Join the Parent-Teacher Association (PTA)

One of the best ways parents can influence school culture is to join the PTA. This organization partners with parents, teachers, and staff to support students. They raise funds for field trips, extracurricular activities, technology, and equipment that may fall outside of a school's budget. They plan events and coordinate volunteers. Their meetings serve as an opportunity to discuss new programs and ongoing issues, such as sponsoring an art class during recess, providing a homework-support program, ensuring car and pedestrian safety, and getting emergency earthquake kits in classrooms.

Many of us lead hectic lives, and it can be difficult to incorporate yet another commitment into already-overloaded schedules, but time is precious for everyone and the more volunteers there are, the less everyone has to do. Plus, there are many benefits to joining the PTA. First, it's one of the most direct ways parents can improve the quality of education and variety of opportunities at a school. Second, when children see their parents putting in the extra effort to volunteer, they realize their education is a priority. Third, PTAs provide an easy way for parents to connect with each other and share knowledge or just commiserate over their babies growing up. Parents are part of the community, and they can help built it, too.

Connect over Learning at Home

When parents show they value education, it has a positive impact on children, since they tend to value what their parents value. How do you indicate that you care about their academic journey? Ask children about what happened at school and specifically what they worked on that day. Of course, frequent answers to these questions include "Nothing," or "Recess was fun," or "The same old stuff." But it's important to dig for more. To get more than stock responses, try inquiring about specific subjects, for example, "What was the lesson in math today?" You may also need to follow up their short answers with statements and questions, such as "Tell me more" or "Can you show me what you mean?"

Reading is another activity that parents and children can share that supports learning. Not only does it provide a quality way to spend time together, but reading out loud also helps children build language skills and stimulates their imaginations. Capitalize on this by allowing your children to see *you* reading for pleasure. Children imitate parents and are more apt to continue reading as they grow up if they see their parents enjoying a book. They need to see that TV and video games are not the only forms of home entertainment, that phones aren't the only source of information. Modeling healthy behavior is an important part of parenting.

Changing the System with the Times

Public schools have been functioning with the same basic structure for decades with little consideration as to whether this structure is optimal for student learning and development. For example, why do most schools still adhere to a ten-month calendar? Why a six-and-a-half-hour school day? To engage in meaningful discussions about school reform, it's critical to examine the sacred cows of our educational system to see what is truly serving students and what has become obsolete or even detrimental to learning.

The 180-Day School Year

Most students attend public school from September to June, averaging about 180 days in the classroom. This schedule originated because generations ago parents required their children to help with farming during the summer, a need that in most cases is no longer relevant to modern society. It's high time to question whether this antiquated approach to scheduling the school year is really what's best for children. There are districts that successfully run year-around programs with students attending classes roughly ten to twelve weeks at a time with breaks in between. Proponents of this approach argue that it increases retention of material and is a more efficient use of school resources.[34] This type of schedule may not work for all districts, but it's worth exploring what style of academic calendar is ideal for student learning instead of blindly accepting a system based on an outdated agrarian past.

Grouping Children by Age

It defies logic to group children by age when we know they don't start off with the same skills and abilities, when we know they learn at different rates, and when the goal is often to hold a particular age group to specific learning standards. For example, some five-year-olds start kindergarten knowing how to count to one hundred and how to write their names, while others can only count to six and may recognize only a few letters of the alphabet. Multiage education, which a few public schools in the US provide, offers a more developmentally appropriate way of teaching children.[35] For example, allowing five-, six-, and seven-year-olds to work toward the same standard—say, adding whole numbers—in one classroom keeps precocious five-year-olds engaged while also giving struggling seven-year-olds the time they need to learn the concept. Multiage education has other benefits as well—it tends to be learner-centric and can help students develop mentoring and leadership skills.[36] Multiage education is one possible approach to appropriately grouping children, and there may be others. Above all, shouldn't we be organizing classrooms according to what supports academic success—not what is most convenient or traditional?

Best Teachers, Neediest Students

Many new teachers leave the profession after a few years due to the stress of the job. Part of the problem is the illogical nature of the system: often new teachers are the ones thrust into instructing the largest classes, the ones with challenging behavior issues, and the widest array of student abilities, while the experienced teacher down the hall gets to teach what he likes, avoiding, say, basic English or just freshmen in general (this is particularly common in high schools). The inexperienced teachers quickly become overwhelmed, and the struggling students do not achieve academic success. Teachers quit. Students drop out or fail. It doesn't have to be this way. The best, most qualified teachers should be working with the neediest students. (Sometimes the most effective teacher is the twenty-year veteran, but other times, it's the relative newbie with only a few years under her belt.) These teachers have the skills to determine what struggling students need and the wisdom to know how to reach them. They have a variety of tools at their disposal, with an intuitive sense of what method is likely to work with a particular student. If the most qualified teachers were consistently working with the neediest students, new teachers would perhaps not burn out so quickly, because they would have ample time to develop their skills, eventually becoming the most qualified teachers themselves.

Class Size

Class size in most American public schools varies between twenty-five and thirty-five students, but is that range ideal? Research on optimal class size is mixed—in results and quality; some studies show a correlation between smaller classes and higher academic achievement, but others don't. However, the consensus is that smaller class sizes *do* provide the most benefit to minority and disadvantaged students, perhaps making class-size reduction an important tool for narrowing the achievement gap.[37]

While small class sizes cannot guarantee each student will reach his or her potential, large class sizes can prevent that from happening, especially since keeping some semblance of order with thirty individuals is much more challenging than with, say, twenty. Students in smaller classes have a better chance of not being lost in a crowd. Teachers have fewer assignments to grade, thus more time for providing individual attention, communicating with parents, and undertaking meaningful professional development.

Length of the School Day

Most children in public school attend classes for about six-and-half hours a day, which is problematic for a few reasons. This schedule is often at odds with the work schedules of parents, leaving them to scramble for childcare when school lets out for the day. The six-and-a-half-hour day often does not provide enough time for recess or enrichment activities like art. Lengthening the school day could alleviate some of the stress on working families. It would allow schools to increase time on the playground (children need to move a lot!) and quiet time spent in the classroom. For example, many schools offer scheduled time for students to read (commonly referred to as Sustained Silent Reading or something similar). Often no more than ten minutes is allocated, which is just when many stories get going. A longer school day could also mean more time for the arts and other subjects that are often perceived as "extras," though they are the ones that typically matter most to students. The decision to add an hour or thirty minutes to the school day should not be an arbitrary one—added time must be used wisely in order for it to be effective—and what works for one district may not work for another, but each district or school should be questioning how the length of their school day is affecting students and families.

Careers, Not Just College

Our education system seems to narrowly focus on preparing children for college, yet not everyone chooses to continue their schooling in this way. According to the US Bureau of Labor Statistics, in 2017 only about 67 percent of high school graduates were enrolled in college.[38] What about the other 33 percent? Some of them graduate unprepared to pursue the next step, perhaps unsure of what that next step is. Some enroll in college—because they feel like that's the only option—and quit when they realize it's not for them.

There are many ways to earn a living that do not require a college degree and are no less valuable or rewarding. Making college the ultimate goal for all students is demeaning and demotivating to those who don't see it as their path. Schools should devote more time and resources toward helping children explore *all* their career options, not just the ones that require a college diploma. Schools should encourage children to find their true calling, whether that's being a car mechanic or a metal artist, a carpenter or a lawyer.

We should be bolstering arts and vocational education in schools, rather than cutting these programs. Students need to experience more than just reading and math and standardized tests—they need to work with clay, design a theater set, use a hammer, replace a fuse, or take a water sample from a stream. Without these types of hands-on experiences, it is difficult for students to determine what may be their calling. The obsessive focus on attending college is also a detriment to the economy. Some sectors, such as manufacturing, are suffering from a lack of skilled workers.[39] Most students are not exposed to nor trained to enter these types of specialized career paths in high school. Children and society both benefit when the public education system provides a variety of learning opportunities beyond sitting at a desk.

Advocating for Change

It's one thing to learn about the educational system, question it even, but how do you go about changing it? The issues discussed in this section—length of the school year, how students are grouped together for instruction, who is providing that instruction, the hours spent at school, class sizes, and the goal of public education—are all topics that parents should bring to the attention of local school boards, district administration, and state education governance.

You can also make your voice heard by being an informed voter. Elect officials and legislators who support equity in education. Legislators are the ones who control the purse strings, and failure to provide adequate funding is a major stumbling block to implementing any change. A University of Washington education professor, the late Dr. Ken Sirotnik, would ask two questions that anyone can ask a policy maker: Whose interests are being served by what you are doing—or not doing? How does this affect student learning? Any official who cannot answer these questions to a satisfactory degree has no business making decisions about education.

As we fight for an educational system that works for all children, it's worthwhile to note that you can't effectively improve the system without taking a candid look at how it came to be, without acknowledging the historical forces that shaped it. There's a quote attributed to George Orwell that says, "The most effective way to destroy people is to deny and obliterate their own understanding of their history."

Truth in History

It is important to be honest about our past and present. Telling the truth about history from multiple perspectives—not just the version espoused by rich, white people—is key to providing an equitable education. For example, wealthy industrialists like Ford (automobiles), Carnegie (steel), and Rockefeller (oil) are often touted as great men who achieved the "American dream," and helped to expand important sectors of the economy, but that's not the whole story. What's not commonly taught is that these "great" men made their fortunes off the backs of child labor, from employees clocking brutal eighty-hour workweeks in unsafe conditions. Students are bound to question what we mean by "life, liberty, and the pursuit of happiness" when they learn that these titans of industry, often characterized as heroes in history books, were the ones who created the need for laws to protect workers in the first place. Similarly, when one realizes that the Native peoples were robbed and murdered by the invading Europeans, that slaves built the South, that foreign policy has been one of aggression for corporate interests, that we have put profit in front of people and the planet, it is no wonder many students grow up to feel disenfranchised, apathetic.

Ronald Takaki, a former University of California, Berkeley, professor, talked about how he couldn't relate to school when he was growing up because it was all about powerful white folks far away, which meant nothing to a Japanese American kid in Hawaii who wanted to surf. It wasn't until one of his high school teachers, also Japanese American, took an interest in him and convinced him to think about college, even wrote a letter on his behalf to a university in Ohio, that Takaki began to put forth any academic effort. Without the intervention of this teacher, he would never have become an influential professor in multicultural education. His book, *A Different Mirror*, is a widely read history telling how minorities played vital roles in establishing the wealth and power that the US enjoys.

Another influential book that should be a part of every high school reading list is *A People's History of the United States* by Howard Zinn. It chronicles the history of our country from the perspective of the people who were exploited in its making. This book stands in stark contrast to most history books, which tend to glorify the people in power and their accomplishments without regard to the fate of those they used and abused to achieve success.

Reading books like Zinn's and Takaki's, along with others written by the diverse voices (authors suggested in the Ethnic-Specific Literature section in Chapter 2) we have in this country, can provide various perspectives on history and encourage students to engage in critical thought. To do otherwise is to whitewash the past; a lie by omission or minimization is still a lie, and once children sense that adults have been lying to them about the basic premises of the country in which they live, it is hard to regain trust. If the truth in history is presented and authentic diverse perspectives that students can relate to are offered, then more honest conversations can happen, learning takes place, compassion is cultivated, and those, like Takaki, who felt ignored, are more likely to speak up and feel like they belong in the classroom. We all need our voices to be heard.

Honesty about this country's history will hopefully not only bring about more academic engagement in the classroom but also foster a culture of integrity and respect within schools, one that overflows into communities. When it is clear that the "American dream" is more readily accessible to certain people, and when a third of students, mostly black and brown, are not completing high school, then "all men are created equal" seems like little more than a catchphrase. If we aren't truthful about how we got here as a nation, then the solutions won't address the real problems in education.

Revamping Schools Boards

School boards are a vital component of our educational system, yet the way many of them function is flawed. Run by democratically elected members of the community, school boards give locals a say in how their schools are run; school boards hire leadership and approve materials used for teaching. However, politics, personality conflicts, ignorance, and power plays often take precedence over what's best for students. For example, the Texas Board of Education decided to rewrite history by changing certain terminology in their social studies standards; the term "triangular Atlantic trade" replaced all references to "slavery."[40] The implication that the forcible capture, buying, and selling of human beings from Africa was a legitimate business is not only wrong but especially demeaning to Black Americans and certainly another reason to distrust what happens in schools.

The Texas Board of Education is not alone in their unsound decision-making. Many school boards across the country have banned books because they contain foul language or depict controversial aspects of society such as racism and sexism. For example, Steinbeck's *Of Mice and Men*, Toni Morrison's *Beloved*, and even Harry Potter books have been frequently challenged or banned.[41] Rather than encouraging teachers and students to have frank, open classroom discussions about controversial words or situations—words and situations many students encounter on a daily basis anyway—some school boards would prefer to sweep these issues under the rug by banning books. Who does this benefit? Certainly not students.

In addition to banning books, school boards can be quite contentious over a number of issues, such as whether to maintain arts instruction, add bilingual education, or close schools with low enrollment. These issues are complex, and sometimes none of the options on the table are optimal, but too often decisions are made based on partisan beliefs and adult egos rather than what best serves children.

One way to make school boards more effective would be to change their makeup. Including educators, parent representatives, and high school students could help keep the decision-making more inclusive, equitable, and child-centered.

Another way to improve the functioning of school boards would be to divide large districts into smaller, more coherent systems that are better equipped to meet local needs. Smaller school districts can feel less overwhelming to parents and teachers because within them it is easier to make personal connections and communicate with one another. A school district with ten schools, for example, has a better chance that the school board will actually interact with staff, families, and students than a district with forty schools, as in one Seattle suburban district. The closer the connection to the community served and its culture, the better the representation. Local input is crucial for running schools that adhere to national goals and guidelines while meeting the needs of individual communities.

Less Emphasis on Testing

Test fever is another aspect of public education that is hindering teaching and learning. We know that measuring progress and success is necessary to ascertain whether a program or system is achieving desired results. Yet test scores are just one part of looking at student achievement. To get a clearer picture of what a person can do, we must look beyond one test. For example, even though SAT scores are an important part of gaining entrance to colleges, the whole admission application is scrutinized —essays, portfolios, recommendations, and interviews provide valuable information about students' abilities. Yet we still examine and then judge the success of K–12 schools mostly through the lens of test scores.

It costs a lot of time and money to look closely at what a person can do academically. The standard tests are useful for providing a snapshot of how a student is doing at any given time. They can also give some insight into how districts, schools, and classrooms are functioning overall. But it would behoove us to remember that knowledge, wisdom, the ability to learn, and love of learning can't be measured by test scores alone. Other aspects of student achievement like projects and daily classroom work can provide evidence of meeting learning standards. Report card grades also provide useful information about student achievement. If we are going to put less emphasis on tests, then administrators and the general public must place more trust in individual teachers, the people who work directly and consistently with students, to objectively assess whether students are meeting learning standards.

However, this is a two-way street: If teachers are to garner more trust, then they will need to improve their performance by being more professional about grading and better understanding assessment. First, grades should be based on how actual student work measures up to the standards—no extra credit for wearing school colors or assuming that kids know how to do something. Second, professional educators will need to develop more expertise in assessment because lack of knowledge is contributing to the inconsistent interpretation of results. For example, it's important for teachers to learn the difference between formative and summative assessments, between achievement tests and aptitude tests. They need to understand and correctly use terms such as test validity, reliability, cognitive demand, and standard deviation. Knowing the lingo matters because the persistent misuse and misunderstanding of testing is crippling morale at schools and impeding student learning. A logical place to start would be to incorporate consistent coursework about assessment in teacher education programs. Unions and districts could also collaborate by providing staff development trainings in how to accurately measure student learning.

Teacher Salaries and Benefits

The classroom teacher is key to the success of students in any school. Unfortunately, there are many highly motivated, qualified people who won't even consider teaching as a career, and one of the main reasons is the low salary. Teachers just don't make that much money compared to other fields hiring personnel with similar education and experience. When a person who loves science and engineering weighs the options of teaching high school science or working in a corporate lab, the difference in starting salaries is stark. A fifteen-year veteran teacher with a master's degree makes roughly the same as a new hire fresh out of college with a bachelor's in science at a technology company. The choice becomes a no-brainer for many—especially when one considers expenses like paying back students loans, supporting a family, or buying a home.

While I do believe that teacher salaries are unacceptable for such an important profession, one that requires so much education and dedication, there is a caveat to this issue: teacher compensation is not as bad as *some* educators make out. (I'm not referring to educators who live in areas where salaries are well below cost of living. There is no excuse for that. No teacher should have to work multiple jobs to make ends meet!) This is important to make clear—and it may ruffle a few feathers. Teachers have gone to great efforts to dramatize the plight of low pay, yet the compensation includes significant benefits—for example, the amount of time off. Besides the usual holidays that everyone gets like Labor Day and Thanksgiving, there is typically a two-week winter break around Christmas, a midwinter break around Presidents' Day in February, and a week for spring break. Then add the weeks off during summer break, resulting in as much as six to seven weeks (sometimes less if a teacher participates in summer school or attends continuing education classes). And the pay comes monthly all year long, not like the varying amounts an hourly worker would see. Also, because teachers are salaried employees, snow days, strikes, and sick days (usually about ten allowed per year, and they can be banked from year to year) do not cost teachers money. Though health insurance coverage for more than the employee means out-of-pocket costs, the district does pay enough for just the employee. So many jobs just don't have all these benefits.

I don't intend for the considerable time off and other benefits to be a reason to not pay teachers more, but it is important to be open about the current situation. As I stated earlier, if we are not honest about what's happening, then public education issues cannot be sufficiently addressed.

Of course, despite the significant benefits, I believe we should double teachers' salaries. Yes, that is a lot, and the only times I've heard of salaries doubling are for athletes, entertainment stars, or executives of major corporations (whose contributions to society are arguably much less significant than teachers'). However, the benefit would be huge.

For one thing, teachers could no longer complain that their salaries didn't provide a living wage. The line, "I don't get paid enough to [fill in the blank]" would disappear. Professionalism would increase with the distraction of low pay taken away, thus more energy and focus on teaching and learning—contributing to a more positive school culture. That focus on the job would also lead to more respect from administration. A good wage also helps spawn pride and positive attitudes, which can be very contagious and motivating for students and other staff.

According to the National Education Association, the average public school teacher's salary for the 2014–15 school year was $57,420.[42] (Average salaries vary widely between states, from $77,628 in New York to $45,218 in Idaho.)[43] Doubling teachers' salaries wouldn't pay for yachts or multimillion-dollar homes, but starting out at around $60K–$70K (like many engineers with a BS) and topping out at around $135K–140K is a comfortable living. In fact, there is one Seattle-area district that has upped their starting pay for teachers in the 2018–19 school year to $63,000 a year, a 19 percent increase.[44]

Another advantage to doubling teachers' salaries is that more people would compete for teaching jobs, increasing the diversity of the staff. One of the many issues I have heard building and district administrators talk about over the years is hiring qualified teachers of color. A staff that at least somewhat matches the student body in diversity has a better chance of becoming a vibrant learning community than one that is only populated by white women. Race is a factor in day-to-day life, and young people of color can often better relate to someone who looks like them, someone who may have lived similar experiences. Having positive, diverse role models can help children from all backgrounds and genders see that education does pay off. Yet the low wages of the teaching profession when compared to other careers is a deterrent for many who do not come from affluent roots;

it's not considered a way up and out of poverty. Higher salaries would draw more talented people from all backgrounds.

Another benefit of more interest in and competition among teacher jobs is increased retention. About 14–21 percent of teachers leave their school every year.[45] In fact, 90 percent of open positions are available because teachers have left the profession, and two-thirds of those teachers have done so for reasons other than retiring—such as career dissatisfaction.[46] Better retention rates would mean that principals would likely not have to face the dilemma of leaving positions vacant or filling them with ineffective teachers. (This is particularly an issue for mathematics and science instructors and special education positions teaching high-needs children—principals sometimes scramble to find qualified teachers for these roles.)

How well public-school teachers are compensated has been and continues to be a sensitive issue. I would guess most people in charge of hiring employees would say offering a lucrative salary attracts more people. More people applying for a position will increase the likelihood of finding the right person for the job. Our children deserve the best teachers, and those teachers should be appropriately paid for their vital work.

Union Support

Teachers unions, like other labor unions, exist to protect employees from unfair and unsafe working environments. For example, they ensure employees are compensated appropriately and undergo due process before being fired. Each school district has local affiliates that are part of state and national unions. School district negotiations with unions vary from contentious to collaborative. The most common and often-heated issue is about teachers' salaries, and one of the benefits of increasing teachers' pay is that it would free up unions to focus on other issues.

With higher salaries, the professionalism of teachers needs to match— and unions could lead the charge when it comes to quality control and professional development. Unions work hard to protect the rights of teachers from whimsical administrative practices, as they should, but sometimes, in doing so, they also go to undue lengths to protect incompetent teachers, which undermines the whole profession. There are way too many teachers out there who shouldn't be working with children.

I believe that unions should be more involved in improving teaching and learning; for example, by collaborating with school districts and universities on professional development and establishing teaching standards. The role of maintaining reasonable workloads and expectations is important, but it shouldn't be the sole function of unions. If they focused more on providing meaningful enrichment for teachers, for example, through coaching, everyone would benefit—teachers would feel less stressed and more supported, and students would receive improved instruction.

Community and School Collaboration

More and more it seems that schools have become a place where societal woes are to be addressed. On top of teaching academics, educators are expected to implement programs about family life, sexual health, bullying, trauma, and social skills. While schools are not responsible for curing all society's social ills, they can be part of the solution. Some schools have successfully collaborated with communities through mentor programs to help increase student achievement.

For example, one fruitful community-school collaboration started in 1988 inspired by New York philanthropist Eugene Lang's "I Have a Dream" Foundation. The GOLD Scholars program offered a class of sixth graders from an inner-city Seattle elementary school scholarships for college tuition if they committed to participating in the program and graduating from high school on time (or within one extra year.)[47] In addition to tuition assistance, the program provided tutoring and mentoring, requiring students to check in daily with a counselor about schoolwork and life. Having consistent support from adults that were not their parents was vital in helping these children develop the social skills and self-esteem that paved the way for their academic success. As of 1994 (the scheduled time of graduation), a majority of the students not only were graduating high school but also were qualified for some sort of education or training afterward. Not every cohort of sixth graders is going to be lucky enough to have a benefactor, but one of the most motivating elements of this program had nothing to do with offering money—it was about developing positive, consistent personal connections with the students, which helped them flourish emotionally and academically. And that's something any community member or group can provide.

Another example of a successful community-school collaboration started at a low-income apartment complex rife with crime and addiction. Many students who attended a school where I taught lived in this complex, and few had a quiet, safe place to go after school to do their homework. The school administration and a university professor applied for and received a grant to pay for an apartment in that complex where structured, supervised after-school activities, led by a credentialed teacher, could take place. Many students received free tutoring or simply enjoyed a dedicated space to study or read. The program was so successful that it was duplicated in other low-income apartment complexes in the area. Unfortunately, funding eventually dried up and the program was discontinued.

Any programs that are grant-funded are precarious in terms of long-term sustainability because grant applications must be renewed, often annually. These types of programs need stable sources of funding to remain successful—such as a dedicated benefactor—and when they are consistently funded, the benefits to both the community and the students can be huge. It's important to take into account community culture when considering collaborations with local schools because what communities value—in addition to the systemic problems they face—will play a significant role in what kind of programs will be effective.

Accept the Challenge

Thomas Jefferson believed that an educated populace was vital to a democratic society. Educated people can think through rhetoric and flawed arguments; make informed decisions, whether it's to buy the newest product or vote for the best candidate; learn from the past; solve problems; and be flexible enough to deal with an ever-changing, diversely populated world. Providing quality public education for all students is an essential part of life in the twenty-first century—and one of our biggest challenges. The situation cannot be fixed with one statement, program, conference, book, or bill. The elements discussed in this book—what is taught, who teaches and how they teach, how learning is measured, who is in charge, what educators learn, and the effects of school and community culture—all play big roles in the way public education functions. Any designs toward school reform should take each of these factors into account. We also must remain open to new factors that arise—the world is constantly evolving, and public education must be dynamic enough to change with it.

I firmly believe that upon graduating high school, every student should feel equipped with the tools they need to embark upon further education or a career of their choosing, whether that person is from rural Arkansas, a suburb in Chicago, or inner-city Phoenix. My hope is that now, after reading this book, you also feel equipped to spark meaningful discussion and take action when appropriate. Just starting the conversation, asking educators and policy makers about what is and isn't working for students is a step in the right direction. All children deserve the opportunity to learn and become vibrant members of their communities. A more knowledgeable society has a better chance of becoming a more just and equitable one.

Endnotes

1 *The American Heritage Dictionary Online*, s.v. "curriculum," accessed September 1, 2018, https://ahdictionary.com/word/search. html?q=curriculum&submit.x=48&submit.y=17.

2 Office of Superintendent of Public Instruction, "Washington State Comprehensive Literacy Plan: Birth to Grade 12," June 2012, http://www.k12.wa.us/ela/pubdocs/CLP.pdf.

3 "How Did U.S. Students Perform on the Most Recent Assessments?" National Assessment of Educational Progress, accessed September 1, 2018, https://www.nationsreportcard.gov.

4 "Selected Findings from TIMSS 2015," National Center for Education Statistics, accessed September 1, 2018, https://nces.ed.gov/timss/timss2015/findings.asp.

5 "School Reports, 2016–17," Seattle Public Schools, accessed September 25, 2018, https://www.seattleschools.org/cms/One. aspx?portalId=627&pageId=6369011.

6 Lev Vygotsky, "Interaction between Learning and Development," in *Readings on the Development of Children*, ed. Mary Gauvin and Michael Cole (New York: W. H. Freeman, 1997), 29–36.

7 Valerie Strauss, "Report: Big Education Firms Spend Millions Lobbying for Pro-Testing Policies," *Washington Post*, March 30, 2015, https://www.washingtonpost.com/news/answer-sheet/wp/2015/03/30/report-big-education-firms-spend-millions-lobbying-for-pro-testing-policies/?utm_term=.546458ddaf97.

8 Smarter Balanced Assessment Consortium (website), accessed September 1, 2018, http://www.smarterbalanced.org.

9 Office of Superintendent of Public Instruction, "Washington State Report Card," http://reportcard.ospi.k12.wa.us/summary.aspx.

10 Kyle Stokes, "Testing Revolt in Washington State Brings Feds into Uncharted Waters," NPR, July 16, 2015, https://www.npr.org/sections/ed/2015/07/16/420837531/testing-revolt-in-washington-state-brings-feds-into-uncharted-waters.

11 "The State of Racial Diversity in the Educator Workforce," U.S. Department of Education, July 2016, https://www2.ed.gov/rschstat/eval/highered/racial-diversity/state-racial-diversity-workforce.pdf; "Fast Facts: Teacher Trends," National Center for Education Statistics, accessed September 1, 2018, https://nces.ed.gov/fastfacts/display.asp?id=28; "Distribution of Teachers by Age and Gender," Organization for Economic Co-operation and Development, accessed February 13, 2018, https://stats.oecd.org/Index.aspx?DataSetCode=EAG_PERS_SHARE_AGE; "Washington State Report Card," Office of the Superintendent of Public Instruction, http://reportcard.ospi.k12.wa.us/summary.aspx.

12 The New Teacher Project, "The Mirage: Confronting the Hard Truth about Our Quest for Teacher Development," August 4, 2015, https://tntp.org/assets/documents/TNTP_Mirage_Executive_Summary_2015.pdf.

13 "Teaching the Teachers: Effective Professional Development," Center for Public Education, September 2013, http://www.centerforpubliceducation.org/research/teaching-teachers-effective-professional-development.

14 "Teaching the Teachers: Effective Professional Development."

15 Jason A. Grissom and Christopher Redding, "Discretion and Disproportionality: Explaining the Underrepresentation of High-Achieving Students of Color in Gifted Programs," American Educational Research Association (*AERA Open*), January 18, 2016, https://doi.org/10.1177/2332858415622175.

16 "Paraeducators: Requirements of Title I, Part A Federal Law," Office of Superintendent of Public Instruction, http://www.k12.wa.us/paraeducators/default.aspx.

17 "Personnel by Major Position and Gender for School Year 2015–2016," Office of Superintendent of Public Instruction, http://k12.wa.us/DataAdmin/pubdocs/personnel/2015-2016_Gender.pdf.

18 "Characteristics of Public Elementary and Secondary School Teachers in the United States," National Center for Education Statistics, June 2018, https://nces.ed.gov/pubs2017/2017072rev.pdf. [this file cannot be found anymore]

19 American Psychological Association, "Ethnic and Racial Minorities & Socioeconomic Status," http://www.apa.org/pi/ses/resources/publications/minorities.aspx.

20 Office of Superintendent of Public Instruction, "Graduation and Dropout Statistics," 2018, http://www.k12.wa.us/DataAdmin/pubdocs/GradDropout/16-17/2016-17GraduationDropoutStatisticsAnnualReport.pdf.

21 National Association for the Advancement of Colored People (NAACP), "Criminal Justice Fact Sheet," http://www.naacp.org/criminal-justice-fact-sheet/.

22 Office of Superintendent of Public Instruction, "Data and Analytics: Student Discipline," August 4, 2017, http://www.k12.wa.us/DataAdmin/PerformanceIndicators/DataAnalytics/DisciplineAnalyticsAugust2017.pdf.

23 Sam Dillon, "Out of Money, Some School Districts in Oregon End the Year Early," New York Times, May 4, 2003, https://www.nytimes.com/2003/05/24/us/out-of-money-some-school-districts-in-oregon-end-the-year-early.html.

24 Sandi Doughton and Daniel Gilbert, "'We Should Be Screaming' with Outrage: State Does Little to Protect Schoolkids from Earthquake, Tsunami," *Seattle Times*, July 13, 2016, https://www.seattletimes.com/seattle-news/times-watchdog/is-your-child-safe-washington-state-does-little-to-protect-older-schools-from-earthquakes-tsunami/;

25 Arthur L. Costa and Bena Kallick. *Learning and Leading with Habits of Mind: 16 Essential Characteristics for Success* (Alexandria, VA: Association for Supervision and Curriculum Development, 2008).

26 Claudia Rowe, "The Push to Find More Gifted Kids: What Washington Can Learn from Miami's Wins," Seattle Times, December 7, 2017, https://www.seattletimes.com/education-lab/the-push-to-find-more-gifted-kids-what-washington-can-learn-from-miamis-wins/?utm_source=marketingcloud&utm_medium=email&utm_campaign=Ed+Lab+12.7.17_12_7_2017.

27 Office of Superintendent of Public Instruction, "Washington State Report Card," http://reportcard.ospi.k12.wa.us/summary.aspx.

28 Jonathan Berr, "Election 2016's Price Tag: $6.8 Billion," CBSNews.com, November 8, 2016, https://www.cbsnews.com/news/election-2016s-price-tag-6-8-billion/.

29 "State of Our Schools: K-12 Facilities," 21st Century School Fund et al., 2016, https://kapost-files-prod.s3.amazonaws.com/published/5 6f02c3d626415b792000008/2016-state-of-our-schools-report.pdf.

30 Ruby K. Payne, *A Framework for Understanding Poverty: A Cognitive Approach* (Highlands, TX: Aha! Process, Inc., 2013).

31 John Gramlich, "5 Facts about Crime in the US," Pew Research Center, January 3, 2019, http://www.pewresearch.org/fact-tank/2018/01/30/5-facts-about-crime-in-the-u-s/.

32 Office of Policy Development and Research, "Neighborhoods and Violent Crime," U.S. Department of Housing and Urban Development, Summer 2016, https://www.huduser.gov/portal/periodicals/em/summer16/highlight2.html.

33 Abigail Geiger, "6 Facts about America's Students," Pew Research Center, September 7, 2018, http://www.pewresearch.org/fact-tank/2015/08/10/5-facts-about-americas-students/.

34 "Research Spotlight on Year-Round Education: NEA Reviews of the Research on Best Practices in Education," National Education Association, accessed September 1, 2018, http://www.nea.org/tools/17057.htm.

35 Stuart Miller, "Inside a Multiage Classroom: Dividing Students by Arbitrary Birthdate Ranges Doesn't Make Sense," *Atlantic*, May 9, 2017, https://www.theatlantic.com/education/archive/2017/05/inside-a-multiage-classroom/525624/.

36 Miller, "Inside a Multiage Classroom."

37 William J. Mathis, University of Colorado Boulder, "The Effectiveness of Class Size Reduction," National Education Policy Center, June 2016, https://nepc.colorado.edu/sites/default/files/publications/Mathis%20RBOPM-9%20Class%20Size.pdf.

38 "College Enrollment and Work Activity of Recent High School and College Graduates Summary," Bureau of Labor Statistics, April 25, 2018, https://www.bls.gov/news.release/hsgec.nr0.htm.

39 Nicholas Wyman, "Why We Desperately Need to Bring Back Vocational Training in Schools," *Forbes*, September 1, 2015, https://www.forbes.com/sites/nicholaswyman/2015/09/01/why-we-desperately-need-to-bring-back-vocational-training-in-schools/#142623e387ad.

40 Amanda Paulson, "Texas Textbook War: 'Slavery' or 'Atlantic Triangular Trade'?, *Christian Science Monitor*, May 19, 2010, https://www.csmonitor.com/USA/Education/2010/0519/Texas-textbook-war-Slavery-or-Atlantic-triangular-trade.

41 "Frequently Challenged Books," American Library Association, accessed September 1, 2018, http://www.ala.org/advocacy/bbooks/frequentlychallengedbooks.

42 "Rankings of the States 2015 and Estimates of School Statistics 2016," National Education Association, May 2016, http://www.nea.org/assets/docs/2016_NEA_Rankings_And_Estimates.pdf.

43 "Rankings of the States 2015 and Estimates of School Statistics 2016."

44 Neal Morton, "Why Teachers in Edmonds, but Not Tacoma, Are About to Get Double-Digit Raises," *Seattle Times*, August 10, 2018, https://www.seattletimes.com/education-lab/why-teachers-in-edmonds-but-not-tacoma-are-about-to-get-double-digit-raises/.

45 Morgaen L. Donaldson and Susan Moore Johnson, "TFA Teachers: How Long Do They Teach? Why Do They Leave?" *Education Week*, October 4, 2011, https://www.edweek.org/ew/articles/2011/10/04/kappan_donaldson.html.

46 Desiree Carver-Thomas and Linda Darling-Hammond, "Teacher Turnover: Why It Matters and What We Can Do About It," Learning Policy Institute, August 16, 2017, https://learningpolicyinstitute.org/product/teacher-turnover-report.

47 Diedtra Henderson, "Dream On—After Tutoring, Mentoring, Counseling and Cash, Whatever Happened to the Class of 1994?" *Seattle Times*, June 5, 1994, http://community.seattletimes.nwsource.com/archive/?date=19940605&slug=1913942.

Acknowledgements

Several years ago, I started writing about my years in public schools after my sister Alice (who I can't thank enough for *everything*) encouraged me to tell my stories. Since then there are many people besides Alice who have supported me in various ways. Perhaps the best parts of their support have been the encouragement and never bugging me about when the book will be finished.

The many wonderful friends who listened to me talk about it and said they liked my stories were very important to my motivation to share. Several of you (it has been so long I am not sure I remember everyone, so this is a group thank you!) read early drafts and said they liked what I was saying, but that it needed smoothing out. Very kind!

To Jessica who helped with organization and clarifying my ideas, I am so grateful. Not only did you help put my ramblings into print, but you helped me visualize that I could actually put a book together. Your enthusiasm for the work has stayed with me.

To the people at Girl Friday Productions, Kirsten who helped me re-organize the material so that it would make sense, flow, and get my points across, my thanks just can't express how important your work was to me.

Anna's ability to get me to write the necessary documents that go with this endeavor. Beth, who guided me even deeper with those and showed me how to put together proposals and clarify how I talk about my book.

Carrie, who took care of the details I had no clue how to handle, has been—and continues to be—adept with small important details, but more importantly, a supportive friend.

Silvia, who referred me to Gail, who really helped me get closer to my voice and then referred me to Meredith.

Meredith, my editor/writing coach and just a fantastic person, not only gave me encouragement for the content of the book, but she was also very skilled at asking why I had certain elements (which usually needed cutting) and whether I could explain something more and how to make it all connect. Her patience with me and her ability to clarify what I hoped to say while still making sure it sounded like my voice was quite the gift. Her support over the last few years helped me persist in making this book come to fruition. I am so grateful for her friendship, belief in the content of the book, and her unwavering encouragement.

Tonic Books people have been wonderful humans, and of course, instrumental in the final details of making this book a reality.

Thank you all!

There have been many educators that I have worked with or learned from—too many to name them all—who have influenced me through their actions, conversations, coursework, and their writings.

I am so appreciative of all the parents and families that I got to know and who supported what I was doing with their children. My life is much richer having gotten to know and spend time with them.

I owe so much to Patricia Lockett, who mentored me while I was student teaching. She taught me so much, including how to engage students and to not let things get out of control. I used her phrase, "Rude, crude, unattractive, and socially unacceptable," often over the years. Her commanding presence and ability to create a positive learning community in a classroom was remarkable. Her wisdom, patience, and expertise were so vital to my growth, but it was her unwavering passion and love for the children and their futures that showed me the importance of the human connection between teachers and students (and parents). Calling my students "my sweet babies" and being able to tell them I loved them came directly from her.

My daughters, Jayne and Melissa, who lovingly let me know that no matter what I thought I knew, I really didn't know anything. I learned so much from them.

And, of course, I am so grateful for the children with whom I got to work, learn from, and share experiences.

Last Day of School

School day 180: Some years it came as late as the summer solstice. Often it would be a sunny day. On this last day, most schools where I taught held an end-of-year assembly, giving out student awards for perfect attendance, band, choir, and academics. Often adults, like parent volunteers, were also recognized for their contributions.

After the assemblies, there was typically a lot of housekeeping going on in classrooms—students cleaning out desks and closets, finding announcements from December and that "lost" book. I would have some word games and puzzles out. Chess would of course be played. Several yearbooks would be circulating for signatures. It would be a very relaxed atmosphere, with a feeling of joyful sadness that the journey we had shared throughout the year was coming to an end.

I always asked the students to provide some sort of written feedback on the year. I also would have some parting words, possibly preaching, for them. "Do your best, you are worth it." "Education will give you choices." "Treat everyone with respect, especially yourself." "Endings are beginnings, and now it is time to move on. Life brings about change. Keeping a sense of humor and a positive attitude will help you handle those changes." And of course, saying one last time to the group, "Y'all are my sweet babies and I will always love you." Then one-by-one I would call them to get their final report card. But they had to give me a handshake or a hug (a few opted for handshakes) in order to receive it.

After they were all gone and the buses had pulled away, I would sit in my room and bawl for several minutes as my emotions flooded out of me. Putting my heart and soul into teaching the children during the year then watching them leave just triggered something inside of me. The rest of the day (students usually were gone by noon), I would be in a joyous melancholy. So much effort and time was put into the year, and soon, it would be time to do it again, but for the time being, I would relax and reflect.

I am so lucky to have found a career that was my calling. I enjoyed more days than not. Though I obviously have many issues with how schools are currently run and structured, and though I wish the system truly was equitable for all students, I am proud to have been a public-school teacher. For me, the human aspect—the relationships I was able to have with students and families and colleagues—is the best part of what I remember. Love and truth flowed. The biggest gift was sharing life with my students.

I am blessed to currently be friends with some former students and I relish in watching them grow and have families. I have had the honor of attending many high school graduations (often with over 20 former students graduating), several college graduations, and a few weddings. One of the hardest and most touching experiences I've had was speaking at the funeral (by family request) of a special girl who passed from leukemia just a few years after she was in my class.

The relationships we shared were genuine, respectful, and loving. The students touched my life in so many positive ways, like the caring I received when substituting one particular high school first period (starting at 7:25am) class multiple times: "Shh, Mr. Green doesn't like to start the day with a lot of noise." Or a whisper of, "The longer we are quiet, the less work we do." (Or so they thought). Like when the question, "Mr. Green, would you like me to help you clean up your desk?" was posed to me several times over the years. (I do tend to make piles of paper on my desk.) Or when my students made a cardboard sign they waved in front of the school for me during Teacher Appreciation Week. It said Mr. Green #1 in big letters. And in not quite as large letters, "Someone who will always be there and listen to you!!!" "FROM YOUR SWEET BABIES"

But it was the experiences, especially the genuine caring and smiles we exchanged every day, that not only motivated me to do whatever I could to be the best teacher I was capable of being but enriched my life beyond what words I can come up with.

My eternal love and gratitude.

The Author

In 1986, Mitchell Green left a successful position in magazine sales at McGraw-Hill to explore a career in education. While volunteering in a run-down, overcrowded fourth-grade Seattle classroom, Green discovered his true calling; he spent the next twenty-four years teaching children and providing instructional support at public schools in Washington State. Green's career encompassed more than fifteen years of classroom teaching— mostly elementary and middle school classes—and seven years of coaching  and staff development at two large school districts. He has served on numerous state-level committees tasked with reviewing learning standards, mathematics assessments, and multicultural education.

Green spent most of his career working at highly diverse, high-poverty, and "low-performing" schools, experiences that laid bare the inequities in the American public school system—and the collective ineffectiveness of reform. He is passionate about addressing these inequities so that all children—regardless of race or socioeconomic background—have access to a high-quality, well-rounded education.

Green's own education was forged at schools in both the United States and abroad. He earned a BA in German language and literature from the University of Oregon, spending one year studying at Eberhard Karls University in Tübingen, Germany. He went on to earn a master of education from the University of Washington (UW) and a program administrator certificate from UW's Danforth Educational Leadership Program.

In 2011, Green retired from his career in education, though he continues to pursue his love of teaching by volunteering at a local school and serving as a Hatha yoga instructor. Green enjoys speaking and writing about a variety of education-related topics, from the importance of the arts in public education to state standardized testing and more. Learn more about him at www.mitchellreesegreen.com.

Awards

Who's Who Among America's Teachers, 2000 and 2004

Those that are selected for the honor of being designated as "the teacher who made a difference" are nominated by one of their former students. Only 5 percent of our nation's teachers are honored in each edition of *Who's Who* and less than 2 percent are included in more than one edition.

Environmental Education Award, 1999

Received in recognition of outstanding contributions to the effort of waste reduction and recycling education in the classroom and beyond.